GROWING PLANTS FROM SEED

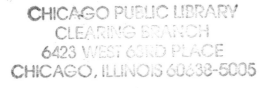

Doc & Katy Abraham

GROWING

PLANTS

FROM

SEED

L&B *Lyons & Burford*

P U B L I S H E R S

Printed in the United States of America
10 9 8 7 6 5 4 3

Library of Congress Cataloging-in-Publication Data

Abraham, George, 1915-
Growing plants from seed / Doc & Katy Abraham.
p.   cm.
Includes index.
ISBN 1-55821-124-1
1. Plant propagation. 2. Seeds. 3. Gardening. I. Abraham, Katy. II. Title.
SB121.A27   1991

631.5'31—dc20   91-37612
CIP

CONTENTS

ACKNOWLEDGMENTS

"To own a bit of ground, to scratch it with a hoe,
to plant seeds and watch the renewal of life—this
is the commonest delight of the race, the most sat-
isfactory thing a man can do."

CHARLES DUDLEY WARNER

FOR OVER FORTY YEARS WE HAVE MADE A GOOD FAMILY
living and gained much satisfaction from growing and
teaching about plants grown from seeds. In our commercial greenhouses and nursery operation we learned
to appreciate what a bargain seed is. A few dollars
worth of seed can generate thousands of dollars worth
of plants grown for ornamentals as well as for food. In
fact, state agricultural college records show that seed is
the smallest item in the cost of growing plants.

Our message is to encourage more and more people (there are already over ninety million gardeners) to get more enjoyment from life by growing their own plants from seeds. We've all learned that energy crunches can create problems. It's smart and healthy to stay off clogged highways and grow more flowers and vegetables, and to maintain a well-landscaped home to shield us from noise and pollution.

Most of the material in this book came from our own firsthand experience. Some came from tips sent us by followers of our newspaper columns and/or radio and television shows. We've tested their ideas and pass them along so everyone can benefit. We would be remiss if we did not share fellow gardeners' tips, and we are grateful for their help.

Another source of good information (and one often overlooked) is seed catalogs. A list of these can be found in the Appendix. The United States and Canada have some of the best seed houses in the world. Their catalogs give up-to-date information on selected varieties and good growing tips for the gardener. Take advantage of their expertise.

We want to express our appreciation to: Harris Moran Seed Company, Ball Seed Company, Jiffy Products of America, Park Seed Company, Southern Exposure Seed Exchange, Johnny's Selected Seeds, National Garden Bureau, the United States Department of Agriculture, Cornell University, Organic Gardening, Bill Taylor, and, for his help with the chapter on houseplants, Ted Marsten.

Special thanks to friends Bob and Mary Jane Mann for helping with numerous mundane details, and to Debbie Allison and Carol Fleischman for their careful scrutiny.

We truly appreciate the enthusiastic support of Chip and Leanna, Darryl, Cullen and Chris, with special mention going to Maureen Abraham for much of the artwork.

We would be remiss if we did not express our gratitude to the countless readers, viewers and listeners who have shared Green Thumb tips with us over the years, and have allowed them to be passed along through our columns, garden programs and books.

DOC & KATY ABRAHAM

INTRODUCTION

IF YOU COULD LOOK INSIDE A SEED YOU'D SEE A SELF-contained living plant, packaged, ready to grow from its embryonic form. Seeds take in oxygen and give off carbon dioxide; they also take in water. They have their own "dinner buckets" (stored carbohydrates), the dynamo that gives them a boost as soon as the temperature and moisture are just right.

Seeds vary in size from the dustlike seeds of orchids (285,000 per ounce) to the *Cocos demer*, a species of Indian Ocean palm (coconut), whose seeds weigh up to forty pounds each.

An odd fact of nature is that there is little relationship between plant size and the size of its seeds. The giant sequoia has tiny seeds (150,000 per ounce) and grows

300 feet or so tall. The common sweet pea runs about 350 per ounce and produces only a delicate vine.

A seed, regardless of its size, is equipped with a "snack bar" called a cotyledon (cottle-LEE-dun), a fleshy rudimentary leaf full of fat, carbohydrates, and proteins. If it has two cotyledons, it is called a dicot. Both cotyledons are hooked to a stem and you'll notice they form a protective hood over the tiny leaf bud. On the other end of the seed you'll find the root tip, forming the first root of the plant as it sprouts. Not all seeds have two cotyledons or "lunch buckets." Some are monocots (short for monocotyledon) having just one cotyledon. The grass family (Graminaceae) are the most important monocot plants in the world. This family includes corn, wheat, rye and all other cereal crops.

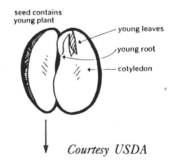

seed contains young plant

young leaves

young root

cotyledon

Courtesy USDA

Starting your own plants from seeds is the most common and cheapest way to produce new plants. Folks who start their own plants from seeds never cease to marvel at what a single seed can produce. Let's take a tiny tomato seed. It weighs only .004 gram, but in five or six months it can grow into a plant that produces 10 to 20 pounds of tomatoes. The seeds in 20 pounds of tomatoes would weigh about 35 grams. In terms of seed, this amounts to about 8,000 percent increase in one generation! From one seed this year, one could produce enough seeds to plant 35 acres next year. If each acre produced 15 tons of fruit, this would amount to more than 500 tons of tomatoes in the second generation.

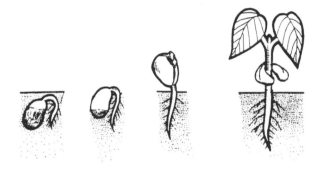

Once the seed germinates (sprouts), a root forms, tiny leaves emerge, and the plant becomes established.

If you want only a few plants, you can buy them from your garden center. But if you use a lot of plants, you might want to start your own. Here are some advantages of producing your own plants from seed.

1. Low cost. Seed is cheap! If you have favorable seed and starting and growing conditions, plants usually can be started at home for far less than they would cost at a commercial grower.

See if anything else you buy can touch seed in price: A 2-ounce packet of bean seeds (between 150 and 200 seeds) at $1.00 means you get one or two seeds for a penny. One packet of lettuce (about 700 seeds) at $1.15 gives you about 6 seeds for a penny. One package of carrots, 750 seeds at $.85, gives you about 9 seeds for a penny. Hybrid cabbage at 200 seeds for $1.90 means about one seed for a penny. Tomatoes, nonhybrids, would be about 200 seeds for a dollar or 2 seeds for a penny.

It doesn't pay to scrimp on seeds. If seeds are translated into plants, the percentage of gain is phenomenal, even after including the cost of fertilizer.

2. You know what you're getting. Some sales people (not usually growers themselves) may recommend varieties not suited to your needs or your growing area. In rare instances, some may change labels. Grow your own and you know what you're getting. (We're not referring to the reliable garden centers or seedhouses, which are conscientious about varieties.)

3. Quality plants are ready when and as you need them. Commercial growers cannot afford to take time to sow a few seeds of a special variety just for you.

4. You can try to grow new varieties (or exotic types) in small quantities.

5. Disease and insects will not be imported from someone else's plants.

6. Growing your own plants can be a lot of fun! Again, we don't want to minimize the good work our com-

mercial growers are doing to produce quality plants for American gardens. They have come up with modern techniques which help the home gardener grow better plants from seeds. Study their methods and you'll soon learn that getting seed to germinate is an art. Even after forty years of growing plants under glass and in the field, we still run into some problems!

1

GETTING STARTED

What Seeds Need

FOUR FACTORS ARE NECESSARY FOR STARTING SEEDS: good seeds, a special seed-starting mix, the right temperature for germination, moisture, and in some cases light or darkness.

The first requirement is viable seed. If you buy seed from a reliable, established seed firm you can be sure the seed is fresh. As soon as you get it, store in a dry, cool spot (40 to 50 degrees F. is ideal) until you are ready to sow.

Garden soil cannot be used for starting seeds indoors. Rather, you must use a relatively sterile mix.

Also, an even germinating temperature of 70 to 74 degrees F. is required day and night. In addition, seeds must never go dry during the germination period.

Light is a factor for some seed (but not all). Seeds of many plants will germinate under either dark or light conditions, but some seeds need darkness to sprout, and others need light. (See Chart 3.1 showing light and darkness requirement of garden flower seeds.)

Most failures in germinating seeds, especially fussy seeds, are due in part to wrong temperatures. In our own greenhouse, we find the best germination temperature for most seeds is from 70 to 74 degrees F. *both* day and night. A night temperature that is too low causes the seed to rot inside the seed coat.

Another reason for failed germination is lack of moisture. Seeds should be kept moist throughout their germination period. One drying out can be fatal to seedlings. A pane of glass or sheet of plastic over the seed flat will keep temperature constant and prevent drying out, but it should be removed as soon as seeds start to sprout.

The elements that lead to successful seed germination are discussed on the following pages.

Ordering and Storing Seed

HOW TO READ A SEED CATALOG A seed or nursery catalog is a storehouse of useful information. Here are a few tips for getting the most from either:

1. Don't go overboard on brand-new items. Some may not be as good as your old favorites, but
2. Don't hesitate to experiment and try new ones.

3. Look for varieties marked "disease-resistant," especially with vegetables. Disease-resistant does not mean the plants won't get any disease. It means they will resist certain diseases. For example, Delicious Melon is resistant to fusarium wilt, but it can get a dozen other diseases that plague melons. Likewise, Heinz 1350 is a tomato that resists both verticillium and fusarium wilts—both bad trouble in most home gardens—but it can get anthracnose and various blights. Some of the resistant types should be grown because there is no other way to fight the disease. Blights can be licked by sprays but soilborne diseases cannot. The letters "V" or "F" after the variety name indicate a disease-resistant variety.

4. Save yourself some money by ordering the larger amounts. For example, if the catalog prices hybrid watermelon seeds at the rate of 10 for 40¢ or 50 for $1.50, get the larger amount and realize a 25 percent saving, a penny a seed. This may sound like small peanuts, but it all adds up when you make out a big seed order. Good seed is a bargain, regardless of its price in a store or catalog.

A common mistake is to sow too many seeds and to make too big a garden or flower bed. A garden plot at least 25 by 50 feet (that's 2,500 square feet) should be sufficient for a small family, but if you have a large family, say five or more, then you'll need a plot 50 by 100 feet or even larger, especially if you want to have vegetables to can or freeze, besides all the fresh ones you want to eat or give to friends. The same rule applies if you're growing annuals for window boxes, urns, flower beds, etc. Plan your seed orders according to the show you want to put on.

ORDERING BY VARIETY Don't buy just any tomato or melon. You buy cars, appliances, pianos by name, so buy your vegetable and flower seeds by variety name. Often you can't buy started plants in a variety you want, but one advantage of starting your own seed is that you can.

Hybrids are a cross between two stable varieties or "inbred lines." The word comes from the Latin *hybrida* meaning "offspring of a tame sow and a wild boar," but a much more common animal hybrid is the mule, the offspring of a jackass and a mare. The spectacular, everblooming, and early mule marigold is a cross between the big American and the little French marigold, and combines American vigor with neat French habit. The plants are unable to reproduce, and not weakened by seed bearing, they bloom and bloom. Germination is below average for these hybrids; you can get at least 25 or more plants from a packet of seed. Because the seeds produced by this cross pollination are lower in percent of germination than regular seeds, the seed companies put more seeds in the packets.

When two selected parents are crossed, the result is an F1 hybrid. The high cost of hand pollination, as opposed to the haphazard pollination by bees, explains the higher cost of hybrid seed. F2 seed is seed that has been saved from the F2 (or second) generation. After the first generation cross, a plant's hybrid vigor declines by about half each generation. F2 seed is cheaper and will give you good plants, but cannot guarantee all F1 characteristics.

MODERN VS. HEIRLOOM VARIETIES

You may wonder which varieties of vegetables have more nutrition—the older or newer ones. Is there a difference?

The so-called heirloom or old-fashioned varieties have no more nutrition than modern varieties, according to studies made by state colleges. However, there can be differences among the same varieties. For example, a biochemist with a seed firm found considerable variations in the amounts of free amino acids in eight tomato varieties, but no uniform difference between old and new varieties. Environmental factors such as soil, weather, maturity at harvest, length and condition in storage, and of course the way it's prepared for eating, can all influence a vegetable's nutrient composition.

Some seedsmen have developed seed banks which save seeds from perishing forever. One company that developed an heirloom business is Southern Exposure Seed Exchange, Box 158, North Garden, VA 22959, operated by Dr. Jeff McCormack and Patty Wallens. They collect and distribute varieties with heritage, flavor, disease resistance, and other qualities of interest to gardeners. Southern Exposure Seed Exchange believes we should have genetic diversity in our food crops, otherwise our whole food supply will be vulnerable to epidemics. They cite the example of the U.S. Corn Blight of 1970. Nearly 80 percent of the U.S. corn crop was planted in hybrids containing a genetic trait that made the crop vulnerable to blight. All the open pollinated (nonhybrid) varieties resisted the blight.

Another organization that deserves credit is the Seed Savers Exchange, 203 Rural Avenue, Decorah, IA 52101. They have an inventory of seed catalogs listing all nonhybrid vegetable and garden seeds in the U.S. and Canada.

COATED OR PELLETED SEED The so-called coated seed is known in the trade as pelleted seed. The idea of coating small seed was to make it larger and more uniform in shape, thereby making it possible to sow the seed more evenly. Pelleting received a lot of publicity a few years ago, but each year you hear less and less about it. Tests show that pelleting delays sprouting because it takes longer for the soil water to penetrate to the germ of the seed, thus slowing the emergence of the plant. Also, pelleted seed costs more.

You'll see a lot of claims made for pelleted seed, but they may not always be justifiable. If you buy well-grown, well-cleaned seed with high germination potential, and are careful about sowing it, you'll get your money's worth without resorting to pelleted seed. However, pelleting does make tiny seeds much easier to sow, and hence, it can save time.

SAVING LEFTOVER SEED If you have saved some of your own seed (or have some left over), store it in an airtight container at a temperature between 35 and 50 degrees F. in a dry, dark place. A good way to remove all moisture is to place some dry milk wrapped in a pocket made of paper handkerchief, or toilet tissue, and secured with a rubber band in the container with the seed. About 2 heaping tablespoons per quart container is sufficient. This absorbs and holds any excess moisture.

You may want to do what many seed houses do to treat their seed—use a fungicide or the hot water treatment. Both protect against soilborne diseases.

The hot water treatment is exacting and should be done by experienced persons. In general, it involves soaking seed in hot water (122 degrees F.) for 25 minutes, then cooling and drying the seed.

The "overcoat" method of treating seed consists of dusting a chemical on the seed. Ask your garden center staff for a fungicide, or use your fruit tree spray (all-purpose type in dry form) and dust the seeds in a container.

SOWING FINE SEEDS A trick many home gardeners use for sowing fine seed is to add Knox unflavored gelatin to the seed. Peat, sand and other inert materials can be used to help in planting small seeds, but the gelatin gives an extra boost by placing water and protein right with the seed. The protein in the gelatin is 16%

nitrogen by weight, so you are actually placing a starter fertilizer solution with the seed. All you need to do is mix some dry gelatin with tiny seeds in a clean, dry saltshaker. Then sow by sprinkling the mix over the top of the starting medium.

Seed-Starting Mixtures

Seeds need a loose, disease-free starting mix for best germination. You can make a relatively sterile mix for starting seed indoors, or you can buy one of the so-called Peat-Lite–type or synthetic soils commercial growers use. These are available in any garden store and many seed catalogs.

Seeds do not need rich soil for germination. The lighter the soil, the better. You can mix your own starting medium or do what commercial growers do and buy brands such as Jiffy-Mix, Grow-Mix, Redi-Earth, Pro-Mix, or many others on the market. These are blends of various materials that provide a loose medium that seeds need for "pushing up." You won't have to sterilize (pasteurize) the commercial mixes—the materials in them are practically sterile.

If you want to make your own seed-starting mix, here's a formula: 1 part sifted garden loam, 1 part peat moss or leaf mold, and 1 part coarse sand. You can also add 1 part each vermiculite and perlite (discussed later) to the blend. Since you're using garden loam, you should pasteurize the blend to kill off harmful soil organisms which cause damping-off and other problems.

(see Chart 1.1). (Damping-off is a disease caused by fungi in nonsterile soil which mows your seedlings down at the soil level.) To pasteurize, bake the soil in a low oven (200 degrees F.) for 30 minutes or so. Allow it to cool before sowing. You can add a very small potato to the soil and when the spud is cooked, you'll know the soil mix is disease free.

TEMPERATURES REQUIRED TO KILL SOIL-INHABITING PESTS

Pest or group of pests	30 Minutes at temperature
Nematodes	120 degrees F.
Damping-off and soft-rot organisms	130 degrees F.
Most pathogenic bacteria and fungi	150 degrees F.
Most insects and most plant viruses	160 degrees F.
Most weed seeds	175 degrees F.
A few resistant weeds, resistant viruses	212 degrees F.

CHART 1.1
Courtesy Ontario, Canada, Department of Agriculture and Foods.

SYNTHETIC OR "SOILLESS" MIXES If you want to avoid a host of problems in getting seeds to germinate, use a mixture of the synthetic or "soilless" materials on the market. These can be purchased separately or already blended. Our advice is to buy a mix with the ingredients described below.

One material in the synthetic or soilless mixes is vermiculite, a mica-like ore heated to a temperature of 2,000 degrees F. until the ore pops into very small particles. This makes an ideal ingredient because it's sterile—no insects or disease—thus eliminating damping-off. It has little or no plant food, so seedlings must be transplanted to soil mixture soon after germination if vermiculite is used alone; otherwise they'll be spindly.

Another material in the synthetic mixes is sphagnum peat moss, obtainable from florists, some swamps, and most garden centers. The other common ingredient found in the mixes is perlite, a volcanic ash which is mined, crushed, and heated to about 2,000 degrees F. until it pops. Perlite has little or no plant nutrients; it facilitates drainage and allows air to get to the roots by creating spaces between the particles. Vermiculite tends to hold moisture and nutrients, whereas perlite tends to release them and provide good air circulation around the roots. Together, vermiculite and perlite, mixed with sphagnum peat moss and fortified with scientifically blended nutrients, make a perfect medium for starting any kind of seed. This mixture can also be used for potting soil and will grow almost any kind of indoor or outdoor plant. See your state college cooperative extension office or a garden center for more information on seed-starting soil. It may make the difference between success or failure.

When planting in an artificial soil mix, make sure it is thoroughly moistened. Apply a high spray at least three times the day before sowing. Waterfog nozzles found in garden stores deliver a fine mist and are excellent for this purpose. Stir the mix to make sure it is wet all the way through. If good drainage is provided in your seedling container (seed flat), there is no danger of overwatering since the mix will soak up all it can hold and the rest will run out. When you are ready to use the mix, apply very warm water so the medium will not require so much heat to bring it up to the required germinating temperature.

Many gardeners like to use Jiffy-7 pellets for starting seeds. These look like a quarter-inch-thick chocolate wafer. Each pellet consists of a growing medium (sterile sphagnum peat moss with plant food added) enclosed in a biodegradable nylon mesh. When you add water, each pellet swells in minutes into a cylinder nearly 2 inches across and seven times its original height and is ready to receive seeds or plant cuttings. No pot is needed, since the nylon net holds the cylindrical shape of the peat moss.

Jiffy-7 pellets for starting seeds or cuttings

To use the pellets, line them in a seed flat or pan so that the edges are touching, then add an inch or so of water to the trays (they soak up warm water faster). When pellets are thoroughly wet and have completely expanded, sow the seed in each pellet. Poke the seed down so it's just out of sight (but not deeply buried). Or, place the seed on the pellet and put a light dusting of vermiculite over it (this works when sowing seed that needs light for germination).

STARTING SEEDS FROM JIFFY PELLETS

1. Place Jiffy-7s in tray that holds water. Gradually add warm tap water to tray. Drain when pellets reach full expansion. (About 1½ inches tall and dark brown in color.)

2. Make small hole in top of each expanded pellet with pencil. Put 2 or 3 large seeds in hole and close with peat. With smaller seeds, press them right into peat surface.

3. Poke a few small holes in transparent plastic bag or plastic wrap and loosely cover tray to form greenhouse effect. Keep expanded pellets at room temperature (70-75°) for most seed types and out of direct sunlight to aid germination.

4. When seeds sprout, remove covering and move seedlings to cooler location with plenty of light— at least six hours of direct sunlight per day. East or south exposures are usually best. This will prevent seedlings from becoming lanky.

5. Snip off all but strongest seedling to allow sufficient room for growth.

6. Water expanded pellets when they become lighter brown. Keep evenly moist, but not soaked.

7. Add *diluted* fertilizer 3-4 weeks after sprouting according to plant type and instructions.

8. When roots grow through pot walls, expose plants to cooler outdoors about 2 or 3 days before transplanting, increasing exposure time several hours each day. This process toughens the plant and prepares it for transplanting outdoors.

9. When transplanting outdoors or in larger pots, plant "pot 'n all" just below soil surface and cover with soil.

Courtesy of Jiffy Products

Jiffy pellets are handy for rooting cuttings, also. The advantage of Jiffy pellets is that there is no need to transplant seedlings—the pellet can be easily tucked into the garden soil at planting-out time.

CONTAINERS The most economical way to start a lot of plants from seeds is to use containers known as flats or seed-starting trays. You can start 300 to 400 seeds in a single flat. There are dozens of sizes and shapes, all with holes in the bottom for drainage. After seedlings are up an inch or so, you "prick" them off by lifting out or transplanting each seedling into a plastic pot, peat pot, or clay pot. Clay pots dry out faster and are more expensive. Plastic pots dry out less quickly, need watering less often, and are easy to use. (See Transplanting Seedlings below).

You can make your own seed flat from discarded lumber, but we suggest you use the seed-starting trays florists use.

Another suggestion is to start seed in or transplant it into "plant packs." Thousands, made from plastic or papier mâché, are discarded each year by people who buy started plants from garden stores. Start collecting them. They last two or three years and are usually free for the asking. Refer to retail and wholesale catalogs for illustrations or go to a garden store and look them over.

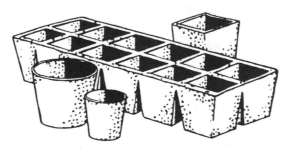

Types of peat pots available for starting seeds

Some gardeners like to start seeds in peat pots made of pressed peat moss. They come in various sizes and must be filled with seed-starting mix. The disadvantage is that they have a tendency to fall apart. They should be peeled off at transplanting time so the sides will not act as wicks drawing moisture from the plants.

Sowing Seed Indoors

Moisten your seed-starting medium (see above for directions), and put it into a container to within one-quarter inch of the top after it is lightly firmed down. If your seeds are difficult to germinate or valuable, sow part of them, saving the rest for a later attempt. We like to dispense the tiniest kinds in a clean, dry, salt-shaker to which has been added some dry play sand or dry Knox gelatin for more even coverage. Gelatin gives an extra boost by providing water and protein. The protein in the gelatin is 16 percent nitrogen by weight, so you are actually sowing a starter fertilizer solution with the seed.

A common mistake, especially when sowing fine seed, is to sow the seed too thickly. Most seed should be at least ⅛ inch apart.

You often see people pouring seed from a packet. This usually causes uneven distribution. We like to pour seed into the palm of our hand, then take our thumb and forefinger and gently rotate a small amount of seed over the soil medium. This gives better control and better distribution.

To sow seeds, pour some into the hand and then gently sprinkle them with the thumb and the forefinger onto the soil medium. You can also sow directly from the packet by holding it with the thumb and middle finger while tapping the packet with the index finger.

Do *not* cover seed too deeply. Fine seeds such as petunia, snapdragon, etc., have little pushing-up power and will rot before they can germinate. Sow thinly, either "broadcast" (scattered) or in rows. Omit covering if seed is fine—just press it into the soil. Coarser seed can be covered with a light sprinkling of fine vermiculite. This prevents drying out and saves you from watering as often. It may not be necessary to cover fine seed if it nestles down in the soil particles and crevices and is firmly embedded. Coarse seed should be covered.

You can hasten the germination process of some hard-coated seeds by "nicking" the large outer seed coat with a file, though don't cut deep enough to damage the embryo. Another trick is to presoak seeds such

GENERAL SEED-STARTING INFORMATION

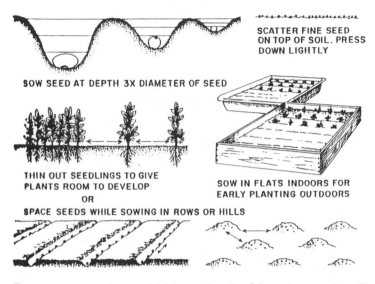

SCATTER FINE SEED ON TOP OF SOIL. PRESS DOWN LIGHTLY

SOW SEED AT DEPTH 3X DIAMETER OF SEED

THIN OUT SEEDLINGS TO GIVE PLANTS ROOM TO DEVELOP
OR
SPACE SEEDS WHILE SOWING IN ROWS OR HILLS

SOW IN FLATS INDOORS FOR EARLY PLANTING OUTDOORS

Do not sow seeds too thickly or deeply. Most tiny seeds will germinate if they are just scattered on top of the soil mixture.

From *Green Thumb Garden Handbook*

as carrot, celery, parsley, morning glory, New Zealand spinach, etc., to omit several days' germination time. Some people pour boiling water over the seed, then drain the seed when cool and mix with dry sand or perlite to prevent clumping. Other gardeners may place slow-to-start seed in muslin bags or socks to soak overnight before planting.

Starch Gives Seed a Jump Start

You can get a two-week jump on the growing season by allowing seeds to grow in soil too cold for normal germination. Professor Roger Kline of Cornell University passed along a technique worth trying:

1. Mix 1 tablespoon corn starch with 1 cup water.

2. Stir while heating to boiling, then allow to cool to a free-flowing gel.

3. Add about ⅛ cup pregerminated seed, pour the mixture into a plastic sandwich bag, and cut off a corner of the bag.

4. Squeeze the gel and seeds into a shallow trench in the garden. Then cover lightly.

Illustrations courtesy Organic Gardening.

Professor Kline says that small-seed crops such as onions, mustard, spinach, lettuce, and parsley work better than large-seed crops such as peas, corn or squash. The gel seeding allows neat planting of sprouts, with less damage and stress than transplanting, and produces better crop stands than bare seeding.

Watering the Seed

After the seed has been sown, whether pelleted or plain, it should be "misted" on the surface with warm water. (A sprinkling might dislodge the seed.) Next, water the seed flat by setting it in a shallow pan of warm water and letting the soil medium soak up mois-

Water seeds with warm water (75–80° F) and keep moist throughout germination. A clear plastic sheet over the seed box will help retain moisture.

ture naturally (this system is called "subirrigation" by college people). This soaks the soil thoroughly and avoids splashing of seed and disease spores which could wreck the seedlings later on. Allow an hour or so for the seed flat to absorb sufficient water. Because the soil has a cooling effect, you should mist or soak with water that is 100 to 120 degrees F.

Then, cover the entire seed flat with a pane of glass, newspaper, or clean plastic sheet. Such a covering conserves moisture, traps needed heat, and prevents drying out of the seed. We like to use a plastic bag over the entire flat. This creates a tiny greenhouse and hastens germination. The plastic frame cover is always closed at night, but during the day it should be raised so heat won't be trapped, especially if the frame is in a small greenhouse or sun room. Experience will tell you how much to raise the cover and when. On a cold, windy, sunless day in midwinter, you may not need to raise the cover at all. But on a sunny day, even though temperatures outside may be below 32 degrees F., your indoor air temperature may be warm enough so that you can raise the cover a foot or more.

If seed or soil becomes dry, immediately syringe with warm water until thoroughly moistened throughout, or place the seed flat in a pan of water, as mentioned above.

We can't stress enough the importance of water to seeds and seedlings. Once the seed starts to germinate, water is critical—one drying out can be fatal! Make sure the soil is kept moist at all times.

Temperature

Place the seed flat in a warm, *not hot*, spot, where the temperature will not go below 68 degrees F. or over 80 degrees F. The magic number is about 72 degrees F., *both day and night*, for almost all seeds.

Maybe you think your house or greenhouse is a nice, warm 72 degrees F. or so. It might be for you, but it isn't for seeds. Here's why: Moisture evaporating from the surface of the seed flat can cool soil by 10 degrees or more. This can bring it down below good germination temperature. Another reason seed flats are cooler than the surrounding air temperature is that quite often water from the tap is as cold as 40 degrees F. in northern regions, and not much higher than 32 degrees F. in winter. Water this cold can lower the soil temperature considerably. So always use warm water.

Tests at the University of Kentucky show that when 40 degrees or 50 degrees F. water was applied to germinating mediums in 65 degrees F. air temperature, the temperature of the seed bed was lowered to almost the temperature of the water applied. And it took four to six hours to get back to a maximum temperature of 62 degrees F. The starting soil usually remained 4 to 5 degrees below the air temperature due to cooling effects of evaporation.

Germination time varies (see seed chart on page 148), but as soon as seeds begin to sprout, remove plastic covering and grow the plants in bright light. It takes heat to make the seed germinate, but after that seedlings can grow at 60 or 65 degrees F. and do well. Check daily to see if mold has formed or if the soil is dry. If a white mold has formed, it means the seedlings are suffering from not enough air circulation or too much water. Put a small electric fan to the side of the seed flat to discourage fungal growth.

We repeat: Check temperature both day and night. Allowing the seed flat to get cool at night is a common cause of failure. A flat set next to a window may get much colder than you realize and seed may rot inside of its seed coat.

USING A HEATING CABLE: Whether you start seeds in a greenhouse, in a window, or under fluorescent lights, the best way to guarantee even heat and excellent germination is to use an inexpensive heating cable. Found in garden stores and many seed catalogs, this could be the best and cheapest horticultural investment you ever make. They are completely safe to use in the home, even with children and pets around. All heating cables are of low heat intensity (3½ watts per foot); they get warm but are never too hot to touch. The cables are waterproofed with a tough plastic coat and may be used in wooden, metal, or plastic flats; on greenhouse benches, in cabinets, or taped to the bottom of glass shelves; installed in wardian cases or miniature greenhouses, in window greenhouses, hotbeds, aquariums, or on windowsills. The cable may be buried in soil, sand or peat moss, or simply spread on beds, trays, or cardboard. Seed flats may be placed directly on the cable. Its gentle heat will provide the necessary warmth for germinating seeds.

Automatic heating cables have thermostats pre-set to

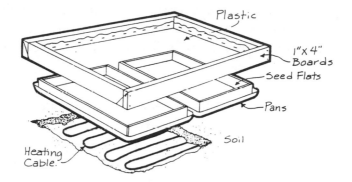

A detailed drawing of a propagation bed. The whole thing is set right into a regular raised bed in the greenhouse and is used to start new plants from seeds and cuttings. Note the heating cable at the bottom.

70° to 74° F. This temperature is ideal for most seeds requiring heat to germinate. The thermostats are in a waterproof enclosure and may be immersed in water, covered with soil, or left exposed to the air. Heating cables without thermostats heat continuously and should be unplugged when the air temperature rises above 75 degrees to save electricity and prevent excessive heat buildup. We suggest using the ones with thermostats. Heating cables with or without thermostats should be handled as follows: Place the outside rows of the cable 2 inches from the edge of the tray, hot bed, or windowsill. Space adjacent rows of the cable 3 inches apart. Cables *cannot* be cut or spliced end to end. Cables must be spaced evenly by looping back and forth to distribute the heat and should never be crossed (see illustration).

In automatic heating cables the thermostat is sealed inside a waterproof capsule located between the heating cable and the lead wires with plug. Place the thermostat between two cable rows at the same depth as the heating cable.

The heating cable should be operated with regular household current (110- to 130-volt outlets). On outdoor installations such as cold frames, we recommend the use of weatherproof receptacles and extension cords for short runs. Consult your electrician for the proper connections for outdoor installations. We recommend that you unplug the heating cable before handling it outdoors.

Indoors the cable may be spread anywhere in window boxes, on plant shelves, and under seed flats. To direct the heat upward, put a layer of Cellotex or Masonite or similar insulating material under the cable. Several layers of cardboard are also effective. The cable can be held in place with electrical tape. A 6-foot long cable is just right to heat 1½ square feet. A 12-foot cable heats 3 square feet. Seedling flats or pots can simply be set in a subirrigation tray on top of the cable. It's also effective to spread the cable in a tray and cover it with a half-inch layer of sand or gravel. The seed flats may then be set in a subirrigation tray on top of the sand or set directly on the sand. We prefer to use subirrigation trays so we can more easily control watering.

STARTING SEEDS UNDER LIGHTS: An alternative to starting seeds in a chamber with a heating ca-

ble is to use fluorescent lights. There are various light fixtures on the market and they all work about the same. A good system for lighting plants or starting seeds is a 3½ foot unit consisting of two 40-watt fluorescent tubes. Don't spend too much time or money selecting tubes since most of them work well for starting seeds or growing plants.

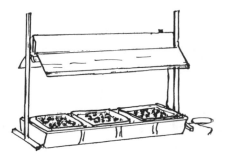

A good home seed germinator can be made with fluorescent lights on adjustable legs. Two 40 watt tubes, 5 or 6 inches above the seed trays, furnishes enough light and warmth for seed germination and seedling growth. In a cool room, polyethelene sheets can be used to enclose the apparatus so a 68–74 degree temperature can be maintained day and night.

Put a thermometer in the trays under lights and maintain a temperature of 72 degrees F. *both* day and night. If you have a space in the basement, you can build yourself a poor man's greenhouse using fluorescent lights. When starting seeds that need darkness for germination, use cardboard or newspapers to cover the tray. (See the charts in Chapter 3).

Seed-Starting Chambers

Our many years in the commercial plant business taught us one thing about getting a good "catch" from seeds. You need a special seed-starting area if you want close to 100 percent success. That's because seeds need controlled temperature and moisture during the period of germination. You cannot maintain an even temperature (both day and night) in your home without a miniature "greenhouse" to trap heat and moisture. That's why we recommend a heating cable or a small box frame with a plastic sheet stretched over the sides and ends. It's worth the effort to build a propagating bed such as the one shown below.

Cold Frames and Hotbeds

If you don't have good indoor facilities for starting seed, you can sow directly in the hotbed or, a little later, in cold frames. Also, these structures come in handy because they can be used to toughen up plants before planting outdoors (see illustration).

If the hotbed temperature can be maintained between 68 and 72 degrees F, it can be used to start seeds. It is best to sow the seeds in containers so they can be removed from the hotbed for transplanting. If built properly, they will stay as warm (and sometimes warmer) than a heated greenhouse.

With a subsoil sandy loam that has good drainage properties, fill the bed to within 5 inches of its final height. Smooth and level the soil. Insert spikes and string heating cable around them. Cover the cable with 1 inch of good garden soil, then remove the spikes. Now you may place seed flats on top or you can fill the beds with 3 to 4 inches of good sowing medium and sow seeds directly into the hotbed. The initial heat buildup is quite slow and we recommend turning the cable on for 24 hours before sowing seeds.

A cold frame, on the other hand, is most often used to "harden off" plants before they are planted in the garden. The cold frame can be covered with glass sash (and sometimes blankets) on cold nights to keep plants from freezing. During the day they are opened if weather is above freezing. Plants get "toughened," or become adjusted to outdoor conditions.

Cold frame

A cold frame is merely a hotbed without heat. Frame construction can be the same, but no means of heating is added. On sunny days it may benefit from the sun.

However, in some areas a closed cold frame may need to be vented to keep it from becoming too warm for the plants. Generally speaking, temperature should not exceed 85 degrees F. for any great length of time.

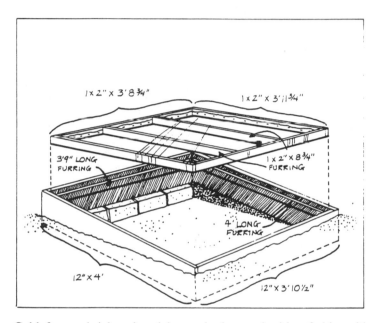

Cold frame: bricks placed beneath the north side of this cold frame give it a 3 inch slope toward the south side to shed rain and catch more of the sun's rays. A heating cable can be added to make it a hotbed.

Home Greenhouses

If you intend to raise a number of bedding plants, think about building or buying a small home greenhouse. There are kinds to fit all budgets. Select a ready-cut type, or design and build one yourself. Make your mistakes on paper first because once the greenhouse is up, it will be costly to make changes.

Now, the popular term for a home greenhouse is "sunspace." A properly installed sunspace can help heat the home. There are some good high-efficiency types of glass which are very effective in blocking heat loss.

Learn from those who already own a greenhouse or sunspace. Here are some considerations:

1. Will the unit be used strictly for growing plants or as a solar room for both living, growing plants and perhaps collecting solar energy?
2. Where will or can the greenhouse be located? For solar collection, a southern exposure is preferred, followed by southeast and southwest exposures. Northern exposures, though least desirable (but not impossible), can take many low light plants, but your fuel bill will be higher because the greenhouse will get less sun.
3. Greenhouses come in a variety of sizes and types, freestanding or lean-to. Custom designs cost more than standard types.
4. Framing materials. Wood and aluminum are both used. If you can afford it, the aluminum with baked-on enamel is great. Redwood materials are available in curved or straight models.
5. Glazing materials. There have been many new developments in glazing for greenhouses. Plastics offer a whole new family in acrylic and polycarbonate; ask about these.

A residential greenhouse or solar room represents a life-long investment. If done properly it can add to the resale value of your home. You can get a lot of comfort and enjoyment from yours, but be sure to do some research before you invest in a residential greenhouse. Ask about zoning laws. Work out the "bugs" on paper before you put down a red penny.

For more information on home greenhouses, write Hobby Greenhouses of America, 8 Glen Terrace, Bedford, MA. 01730. You may want to join Hobby Greenhouses of America, a nonprofit organization. You can also write to National Greenhouse Manufacturers, 1001 South Pine Street, Box 567, Pana, Illinois, 62557.

Sowing Seed Outdoors

Let's familiarize ourselves with garden soil. It's more than just dirt! The soil around your home and in the garden is full of life. If you went out and scooped up a teaspoonful of it, you'd have as many as 5 billion living organisms in your hand. Keep these helpful workers happy with soil management.

Are earthworms valuable to the home gardener? *Yes,* especially in clay, gumbo soils. They help build up topsoil, aerate soil, and allow rainwater to seep down where it's helpful. As part of their digestive process, earthworms take organic matter down and mix it with subsoil. Dead earthworms release about 40 to 50 pounds of nitrogen to the acre. Should you "plant" earthworms in your garden? No, they are already there if you give them organic matter. Keep on adding organic matter (plant refuse) to the soil and the worms will continue to multiply.

When you sow seed indoors, you have better control of heat, light, and water needed for germination. Sowing seeds outdoors is a bit different, but not difficult. Here are some rules to follow:

1. Never sow seed in a cool, wet soil. Wet soil dries to a crust that will be difficult or impossible for seedlings to break through. Seeds will rot quicker in a cold, soggy soil.
2. Avoid planting seed too deeply. There is greater danger of making plantings too deep, than too shallow.

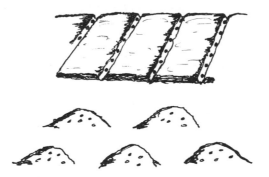

Sowing seeds in rows and hills

Vegetable gardeners plant seeds in either drills or hills. A drill is a single row of plants spaced more or less evenly. A hill is a cluster of plants, not, as the word implies, a mound of soil. You put four or five seeds in a hill and thin them to two or three plants. Never plant seeds in a mound of soil as it will dry out faster than level earth. Seeds most often planted in hills include melons, cucumbers, squash, pumpkins, and sometimes corn.

Wherever you live, plant root crops such as carrots, beets, parsnips, and rutabagas whenever the soil and weather are cooperative. In northern states, root crops can be planted in late May, June, or early July, depending upon the variety. Cucumbers can be planted as late as the first of July for good crops. Early varieties of sweet corn planted as late as July 20 should give you fall corn, barring heavy frosts. Bush snap beans can be planted at 2-week intervals until the middle of August. Late cabbage, broccoli, and savoy set in the first of July will produce good fall crops. Chinese cabbage seed sown at the same time will make sound heads by early fall. (See Chart 2.2.)

Timing Seed Sowing for Outdoor Planting

One of the biggest problems greenhouse operators and hobbyists have is knowing when to start vegetable and flower seeds for outdoor planting, especially in regions where spring frosts come late in the season. It's not so much of a problem in warmer regions of the country. If you live in an area where spring frosts threaten your outdoor crops in late May or early June, it's not a good idea to start your plants too early.

You can gauge your seed-sowing dates according to

the dates you are able to set transplants outdoors. For example, our traditional outdoor planting date in western New York State is Memorial Day weekend, an approximate planting date for much of the upper third of the United States. If your outdoor planting date is in this range, start such items as tomatoes, peppers, and eggplants about 8 weeks earlier, or about April 1 to April 15. Keep in mind that some items, such as peppers, are slower to germinate, so start them at least 8 weeks in advance of outdoor planting time. Remember that weather plays an important part when it comes to setting plants outdoors. In the north, it's common to have frosts early in June and there's no way to predict when they'll come. Listen to your weatherman's frost predictions.

Seedling Care

Just as soon as about 90 percent of the seeds have germinated, remove the plastic covering and move the seedlings from the propagating area flats to a spot on the greenhouse bench that is somewhat protected. If you enclosed each seed flat in a plastic bag or put a pane of glass over the flat as previously described, remove the glass or plastic as soon as seedlings are up. We've found that if we leave them under the plastic, the seedlings get limp and spindly. If the flats are beginning to dry out, then they should be set in a pan of warm water and subirrigated for a half hour or so before moving them onto the bench. Do not water from above unless you're extremely careful. Avoid getting water directly on the seedlings. Seedlings must have good air circulation to avoid damping-off disease (see below), so you should have a small fan going at all times. It should not blow directly on seedlings, and should be placed far enough away so that when you place your hand near the seedlings, it receives only a gentle breeze.

Controlling Insects on Seedlings and Transplants

Below are some homemade sprays we have found to be helpful in controlling spider mites, whiteflies, aphids, fungus gnats and thrips. They are not effective on cutworms or slugs. Cutworms can be thwarted by putting cardboard or foil collars around the base of stems of transplants or seedlings. Slugs are night marauders. They can be spotted with a flashlight, then sprinkled with salt or lime from a saltshaker (be careful not to sprinkle it on the plant). Also, inverted citrus skins attract them. These can be collected each morning when the pests can be disposed of. See chart 1.2

Homemade Sprays

Many home gardeners are reluctant to use chemicals to fight insect pests. We hope the non-chemical methods listed here will help those interested in the organic way to banish pests. Non-chemical methods for coping with

COMMON INSECT PESTS OF SEEDLINGS AND PLANTS

Here are a few pests that might bother your seedlings and transplants. There are other pests which your county agent or extension specialist can help you with.

	RED SPIDER MITE	GREENHOUSE WHITEFLY	APHID
DESCRIPTION	Tiny, almost invisible pest.	Small, white fly; found in groups on the plant's foliage.	Small, soft, pear-shaped body, long legs; red, brown, green and black varieties.
SYMPTOMS	Plant weakens; leaves become brown or yellow and then fall.	Leaves turn yellow and fall.	Plant growth is stunted; distorted buds and leaves. Plant weakens.
LOOK FOR	Webs that can be seen with the naked eye. Mottled and distorted leaves.	White flies on foliage and undersides of leaves; they fly off in cloud when disturbed.	Curled, yellow leaves. Aphids attach themselves to new growth, flower buds; can be found on any part of the plant. They suck plant juices.

Chart 1.2
Courtesy of Darryl Abraham Sign and Landscape

FUNGUS GNATS	CUTWORM	THRIPS	 SLUGS AND SNAILS
Tiny black mosquito-like flying insect. Larvae threadlike, white, with black heads.	Greasy looking gray, brown or black worm; about one inch long.	Tiny, hairy pest; brown or yellow.	Snails have hard shells, slugs have no shells.
Plants may lose vigor and lack color as larvae feed on roots when they occur in large numbers.	Plant broken near soil surface. The climbing cutworm cuts stems.	Discolored or deformed flowers; broken stems.	Night feeders, eat holes in leaves. Leave unsightly mucous track.
Large numbers of slow flying black adults. They usually feed on organic matter, and lay eggs in soil.	Some cutworms hide in the soil by day and feed at night. Others climb on the stem of the plant.	Damaged leaves and flower petals. Thrips chew on undersides of leaves and stems. Threadlike marks on stems.	Chewed foliage, slimy trail.

(

insects are more widely accepted today than ever before, and in many cases they work just as well as the high powered pesticides. For the latest chemical controls, consult your State College, U.S.D.A., or your local Extension Agent.

A note of caution: When using any organic sprays (such as hot pepper, etc.) do not breathe the fumes and do NOT spray on a windy day. It can be irritating to eyes and nose. Also, when using any spray with tobacco, do not breathe fumes or leave tobacco "tea" water where anyone might ingest it. It is deadly toxic as are all tobacco products.

1. TOBACCO TEA. Soak cigarette and cigar butts or chewing tobacco in water until color of strong tea. Can be used as a drench to kill soil insects or sprayed on leaves of plants to kill leaf-chewing pests and aphids. Should be strained through a fine sieve before adding to sprayer. Not recommended for spraying on edible plants. (see above precaution)

2. LIQUID DETERGENT ALCOHOL SPRAY. Mix 1 teaspoon of liquid dishwashing detergent (any well-known brand—*not for automatic dishwasher*) plus 1 cup of rubbing alcohol (around 70%) in 1 qt. of water. Test on a few leaves first to make sure no harm is done to sensitive plants. Spray top and bottom sides of leaves, or if plant is small and is potted, invert it in a large pan of solution (holding soil ball securely) and gently swish back and forth. Repeat in 7 days.

3. LIQUID DETERGENT—HOT PEPPER SPRAY. Steep 3 tablespoons dry, crushed hot pepper in ½ cup hot water for half hour, strain out the particles of pepper, and mix solution with the liquid detergent formula mentioned above. Good for a number of insects bothering both indoor and outdoor plants. NOTE: Have the plants outdoors to apply. Do NOT use on windy day. AVOID breathing fumes. Can be irritating to nose and eyes. You can substitute hot Tabasco sauce or Louisiana Hot Sauce in above.

4. COOKING OIL. Now, a natural oil is being recommended by USDA entomologists. It consists of one cup of a vegetable cooking oil—corn, cottonseed, peanut, safflower, soybean, sunflower, etc.—with one teaspoon of liquid dishwashing detergent (Joy, Ivory, Palmolive, etc.). The oil detergent mixture is added to one quart of water and should be applied every 10 days. A lower rate is advised for cauliflower, red cabbage, and squash plants to prevent leaf burn. Apply it to a "test" plant to see if any burning occurs.

Insecticidal soaps such as Safer and Murphy, mixed according to directions on the label, are being used by many gardeners. The Ringer Corp. in Minnesota, a longtime manufacturer of organic fertilizers and natural pest controls have added Attack brand as well as Safer to their product line.

Many seeds germinate only to succumb to a condition known as "damping-off." Seedlings lop over at the soil line, as if mowed by a scythe. Caused by a group of fungi, the best way to prevent damping-off is to keep a small fan going at all times in the seedling area. It should not blow directly on seedlings but just above or to one side. This dries damping-off spores so they cannot attach themselves to plants. It is a good idea to keep the air circulating all during the time the plants are growing indoors. Take care not to sow seeds too thickly. Thick seedlings are an invitation to damping-off. Have a small fan blow gently on the seedlings to improve air circulation. Air movement does more to prevent damping-off and other diseases than anything else.

After the seeds are up and growing, all they need is bright light, a uniform supply of water, and a cool temperature of 55 to 60 degrees F. at night. They don't need the heat that was necessary to make them sprout. After the seedlings are big enough to handle (about an inch or so tall), you can transplant them into peat pots, homemade wooden boxes, fiber or plastic containers, plastic or clay pots, or whatever is available. They need a loose soil mixture. Equal parts builder's sand, sphagnum peat moss, and clean sifted garden loam is a good mix. Some gardeners add a little perlite or vermiculite to make a looser mixture. Remember, too, that seedling plants are 90 to 95 percent water, so don't let them get bone dry, and make sure they are in a good soil mixture that drains well.

If you transplant into pots, remember clay pots dry out 2 or 3 times as fast as plastic pots because they are porous. Therefore, they need to be watered that much oftener. New clay pots can dry out twice as fast as older, used pots.

Most beginning outdoor gardeners make the mistake of sowing too thickly. This makes it necessary to thin seedlings by hand—one of the most important (and also neglected) garden operations. Thinning is hard work, but it's necessary because it's difficult to sow small seeds far enough apart to allow plants to grow best. If you don't thin plants, they become weeds to themselves, competing for moisture and nutrients. Thin when seedlings are small (about 1 inch high) and soil is moist (but not soggy) so they can be pulled out easily without injuring the remaining plants. For example, onions from seeds can be left in the ground until those that are going to be thinned out are large enough to eat. Carrots should be thinned when they are 2 or 3 inches tall, so as to stand about 1 inch apart. Pull surplus beet plants when they are 4 or 5 inches tall and use the greens. Remember, each beet seed has four or five seeds in a cluster and that's why beets should be thinned more than once. Plants thinned from the turnip row can also be used for greens.

Transplanting Seedlings

If seeds are sown in individual pots or pellets, no transplanting is needed. However, if grown in a container, you'll need to transplant the seedlings into a bigger container—called "pricking off" in the trade. Transplanting begins by lifting out a bunch of seedlings and separating them. The best way to do this is to cut out a block of seedlings and gently separate them one by one. The soil should be just moist, but not soggy; then the block of seedlings can be lifted out intact but separated easily without breaking roots. This is one reason a loose Peat-Lite–type mix is so important for starting seeds.

Separate seedlings by carefully "teasing" them apart so as not to break tender roots.

Make holes in the transplanting mix with your finger or a dibble (a wooden stake or thick pencil). Roots should be set in so seedlings are not overcrowded, and soil gently tucked around each as you go. Seedlings must be watered thoroughly as soon as you have finished transplanting each dozen or so. An inch or so between seedlings is usually enough if they are going to be set out in the garden within 4 or 5 weeks.

Do the job on a cloudy day, if possible. When a flat or container has been filled with newly transplanted seedlings, moisten them with a sprinkling can with a fine mist head. This settles each seedling. They may wilt at first but they will perk up after a good watering. Keep them out of direct sun for a couple of days. And, do not feed them until they are perky.

One of the secrets of good garden transplants is to not allow the young plants to get "soft" from too high a temperature. This often happens if the temperature is above 72 to 75 degrees F. One way to toughen up transplanted seedlings (called "hardening off") is to move the transplants after a week or so into a cold frame (discussed above). Here the young plants get less water and a lower temperature, which checks growth and hardens cells walls.

If you don't have a cold frame, place the plants outdoors in a sunny spot on favorable days and bring them back in each night. Their growth slowed down, the seedlings are better able to withstand the shock of being transplanted into the garden.

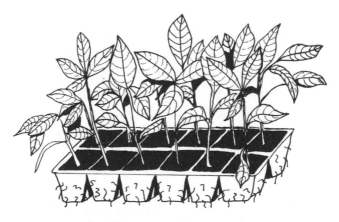

Seedlings started in peat pots

Nearly all transplants can be grown in pots or boxes for 4 or 5 weeks, after which they can be set outdoors. Seedlings however, should be transplanted within a couple of weeks or so. Don't wait too long to transplant your seedlings, as they are apt to get too tall. If you find they are growing rather fast after sprouting, move them to a cooler location and keep the plants somewhat drier to check growth, though never so dry that they wilt.

Transplanting Seedlings Outdoors

Now that you've gone to the trouble of starting seeds in your home, you'll want to set some in the garden or in outdoor containers. Here's how to go about it:

1. Harden plants as mentioned above.
2. Plant after sundown or on a cloudy day if possible.
3. Before transplanting, be sure soil is moist, not bone dry. If plants are in plant packs, they can be pushed out intact by putting thumbs on upper sides of each end, with fingers underneath the pack. The soil block is pushed up, and the seedlings gently eased apart, one by one. Try to keep as much soil around roots as possible. If you use cell packs, pushing individual plants out is a simple matter.
4. The holes for the plants should be slightly larger than the soil ball and roots. If the soil ball is moist you can usually "tease" the plant, soil ball and all, out of the container. Set it in a little deeper than it

was in the original container. If plants are in a plastic or clay pot and are a bit stubborn in coming out, tip the pot upside-down and gently tap its edge against a hard surface. The soil ball will be jarred loose and lift right out, or fall out into your fingers.

5. If plants are growing in individual peat pots, set the pot in the soil an inch or so below soil level. If the peat pot is exposed, even half an inch above the soil, it acts as a wick and the transplant will become dehydrated. You can plant the peat pot and all, covering it completely with an inch or so of soil. If peat pot edges are above the soil in the pot, you can tear or cut them before planting in the soil.

A plant started in a peat pot, ready to be set out in a garden.

6. After the plant is set in the soil, add a little more soil and then add water to settle it. There's no point in packing the soil with your hand or foot. Before you finish the job, add more soil and give a final thorough watering.

7. Weather or other factors may delay outdoor transplanting and your transplants may get tall and "leggy." Some transplants can be made more stocky by "pinching." Use the thumb and forefinger fingernails to pinch out an inch or so of the top of the plant. This causes side buds to develop and makes the plant more bushy. Some plants that respond well to this operation are snapdragons, petunias, coleus, impatiens, and stocks. If tomato plants get tall and spindly they can be set several inches deeper with just the tops sticking out.

8. During cool spells you may need to cover outdoor seedlings and transplants. Garden supply stores and garden catalogs have a variety of protective covers for northern gardens.

Row Covers

There are several ways to protect "touchy" items from frosts in the spring and fall. New polypropylene row covers open like an accordion and expand to about 7 feet by 20 inches. They let light in and hold warmth while insulating tender plants from wind or cold. They last for many seasons, and are a new way to extend your growing season cheaply.

"Hotkaps" are weather-resistant waxed paper "tents" that protect early plants or seeds against frost, rain, wind and insects.

There's also a "garden blanket" that can speed plant

growth and can be used to help grass seed get a faster start.

Homemade covers can be crafted from gallon plastic jugs with bottoms removed.

Planting Seeds by the Moon

One of the toughest and most frequent questions we get is, Should I plant seeds by the moon? Some people call it folklore; some people swear by it. When you consider how the moon influences bodies of water, it's not too far-fetched to believe that the moon does have an influence on seeds. If the moon exerts a force that raises groundwater as it does the ocean tides, we can see how it brings nutrients from the roots to the leaves and causes growth. State college studies show that seeds do take in water and germinate on a regular cycle that coincides with the lunar month.

How do gardeners plant by the moon? During the first two quarters, beginning with the appearance of the new moon, the moon is growing, or "waxing." Gardeners say that's the time to plant or transplant above-ground crops—leafy vegetables, grains, cole crops, parsley, peppers, and cucumbers. They say that the third quarter, when the moon begins to wane, is the time to plant root crops. People who moon plant advise against planting anything during the last quarter. They believe that's the barren time, best for weeding and cultivating. If you really want to get into the science of moon planting, consult your farmer's almanac or feed store calendar for precise timing of the moon's phases. Meanwhile, keep an eye on weather reports furnished by your radio or television news programs.

VEGETABLES

FEW ENTERPRISES AROUND THE HOME GIVE satisfaction and as good a net return as the vegetable garden. State college studies show that for the time spent in the garden, you get a net return of from five to seven dollars an hour. Also, you get an added bonus of high quality crops picked right in your own backyard, when you want them. A well-managed plot 25 by 50 feet (1,000 square feet) should be sufficient for a small family's eating needs, and will yield excess for freezing and canning. Even less space is needed to grow the same amount of food if tomatoes and vine crops are grown on trellises.

For an indication of the value of vegetables in the diet, scientists studied the food habits of people in the

Caucasus Mountains on the eastern shores of the Black Sea. According to an article in *National Geographic* magazine, the number of active people over 100 years of age in this region is estimated at 5,000 (and a good disposition seems to be a common characteristic among the older people). Significantly, over 70 percent of their diet is of vegetable origin, particularly lettuce, cabbage, beans, spinach, corn, celery, and parsley. Corn mush eaten with red pepper sauce and fresh green vegetables are a major part of every meal.

We all know that the fresher the vegetable, the tastier it is—a solid argument for growing your own. And if the American economy takes a dip, you can have a depression-proof garden.

Produce from your own backyard is high in vitamins and nutrients, but it isn't generally known that different parts of vegetables differ in nutrients. The leaf

parts of collards, turnips, and kale contain many more vitamins than the stems or midribs (but even these parts have some nutrients and are good for roughage). The outer green leaves of lettuce are more coarse than the inner leaves but they have higher calcium, iron, and vitamin A value. The core of cabbage is high in vitamin C and so are cabbage leaves. Broccoli leaves have higher vitamin A content than the stalks or flower buds. If broccoli leaves are tender, why not eat them? To conserve nutrients from the vegetables you grow, keep the crop cool and moist until you can prepare them. And when you boil vegetables, don't throw out the water. Use it for making soups, stews, gravies, etc., because the water is loaded with vitamins. Whenever we make bread or pizza crust, we use at least a cup of potato water instead of plain water. It makes the bread more tender and moist as well as more delicious.

When harvest season rolls around, pick vegetables at their proper stage. Try to pick them just before you are ready to prepare them. Cook vegetables as little as possible, preparing them in their skins if you can. If you do peel vegetables, just scrape or pare them thinly. By following the above advice, you will get more mileage from the seed you sow.

How Much Seed to Sow

If you are gardening for the first time, don't bite off more than you can chew! Plan your garden according to the space available, the size of your family, the time you have to work your garden, and the types of crops that please your palate. Remember, regardless of the amount of space you have, you can have a garden. There are many gardens on rooftops in New York City. Where space is a problem, stick to salad greens, a few onions, and a couple of tomato plants. If you have space that adds up to about 300 square feet, then you can add beans, beets, carrots, and more tomatoes. One of our plots is about that size and we grow all these, plus a dozen pepper plants, several herbs, and extra onions in the holes of cement blocks surrounding the area. We also have four half-barrels, one at each corner; we grow tomatoes in three of these and "burpless" cucumbers in the other. Oil drums cut in half and washed clean are fine substitutes for barrels, but be sure you have seven or eight holes drilled in the bottom for drainage. After our beans have stopped producing (we make two sowings to stretch their season), we pull them up and sow turnips and Swiss chard. This is called double cropping.

If you have a plot that is 40 or 50 feet square or more, you can plant corn with squash in among the corn rows. You can squeeze in more if you handwork your garden (machinery makes wide rows) and use mulches to keep weeds down. It makes no difference which way the rows run, although lengthwise rows are easier to cultivate. If rows run east to west, plant your large crops on the north side of the garden so that they will not shade the small crops. You don't *have* to plant in rows. Plant in any pattern that suits your space as long as you leave room enough to walk between groups of plants for weeding and harvesting.

Remember that all vegetables need at least six hours of sun daily, so if your yard is shaded, take note of the amount of sun each spot gets before you order seed or plant your garden. Some folks get around this problem by planting in containers set on movable platforms or pots.

Save Space—Grow Vertically

If you have a wooden or metal fence, you can grow climber vegetables such as cucumbers, tomatoes, melons, squash, and pole beans on it. You can also grow these types of vegetables around trees and let them climb up the branches. The trees should have a narrow base and branches close to the ground, such as an evergreen or clump birch. We have grown buttercup squash and cucumbers in this manner by setting the plants at the edge of the branches so they have full exposure to the sun. First vines may have to be fastened with wire or cloth twists, and melons would have to be supported with slings of discarded nylon stockings. Be sure to keep the plants watered, as the trees take up a great deal of moisture.

All of this is another way of saying: Everyone can have a garden, regardless of income, size of property, or location.

Gourmet and Exotic Vegetables

Many gardeners in the 1990s want to try something different from the regular bean-corn-tomato fare everyone grows. Luckily, today's gardener has the largest selection ever. We've learned to develop a taste for vegetables from every nationality on the globe. Our supermarkets carry gourmet vegetables our parents never saw. Fashion among chefs changes as it does with clothes designers—and the trend is called "Nouvelle Cuisine," or new cooking. Even heirloom varieties are being rediscovered for their superb culinary tastes.

Space prevents us from listing all the vegetables which go into the Nouvelle Cuisine, but there are some excellent seed catalogs which list them and give cultural hints. You can try the exotic types but don't go overboard at the risk of neglecting our native North American vegetables.

We've grown some of these foreign introductions and they include:

Arugula (Garden Rocket). Leaves have a sharp, spicy taste. Much used in France. Make several sowings for continuous crops.

Bok choy or Chinese pac choy (*Brassica chinensis*). A warm weather vegetable that can be grown spring to fall. There are several choys and all are similar in culture.

Celtuce. Originated in China and has the combined virtues of celery and lettuce. Young leaves used in salads. Center stalks used like celery.

Edible chrysanthemum or Shungiku or chop suey green. Ready to harvest in 80 days. Cut plants when quite small for best taste.

Cos or Romaine. Also called Paris White Lettuce. Crispy, with piquant flavor. Head upright, tightly folded and leaves have endive-like flavor. Resists hot weather, when many salad greens wilt badly.

Ground-cherry or husk tomato (*Physalis pruinosa*). Matures in 75 days. Small yellow fruits in parchment-like wrappers. Tasty fresh, in pies or jam. You might consider a close relative, tomatillo (*P. ixocarpa*) with 2 inch diameter fruits when green. Ideal for salsa verde, or green sauce. Has papery husk. Fruits freeze easily.

Chicory (leaf chicory) or radicchio (pronounced "rad-DICK-ee-oh") has a tangy flavor combined with lettuce. There are different kinds and colors—red, green, and beautifully variegated. Some are loosely wrapped, semiheaded, and some tightly wrapped.

Mustard (Giant Red) has attractive savoyed leaves, deep red color or plain green. A cool season plant, ideal for spring and fall salads. Culture: all of the gourmet vegetables are easy to grow. They like a loose, well-drained soil, at least 6 hours of sunlight, plus a uniform supply of water. Sow seed directly into the garden,

making sure you don't cover too deeply. Avoid thick sowing. Later when seedlings are up, you can thin out the plants and use them in salads. Be sure to water during dry spells.

The above list of different, exotic or "gourmet" vegetables is far from being complete. We mention them to pique your appetite. If you wish to pursue something different, study seed catalogs listed at the end of this book. Remember, some members of your family may not have the taste you have for gourmet veggies and that is why we like to repeat: Try a few on a small scale, and stick with your regular varieties, such as the ones that follow.

Asparagus
(ASPARAGUS OFFICINALIS)

Asparagus

Every home should have a small asparagus patch. It's a high-priced item in the stores.

HISTORICAL FACTS: Asparagus has been growing in gardens for a little over 2,000 years. It's a member of the lily family. Before asparagus was used as a food

it had quite a reputation as a medicine for almost anything from the treatment of a bee sting to curing a bad
toothache. The Greeks collected asparagus only from
the wild but the Romans, as early as 200 B.C., gave detailed instructions for the cultivation of this plant.

STARTING SEED: Soak the seeds for 24 hours in
warm water, then plant them. Allow about two seeds
per inch. Cover with loose soil a half-inch deep. Thin
seedlings to 2 inches apart. You can put the extra seedlings in pots. To allow for root growth, plant one in a
6-inch pot or plant in equal spaces right in the ground.

Asparagus is unique among our vegetable crops in
that it has both male and female plants. That's why you
find seed only on about half the plants—the pistillate
or female plants. Male plants yield about 25 percent
more stalks than female plants. Some people wonder if
it wouldn't pay to plant a patch entirely with male
plants and in that way obtain a higher yield. This
sounds feasible, but there is a hitch. Higher yields of
male plants are usually offset by a decrease in the size
of spears. In other words, male plants yield more stalks,
but female plants have larger, fatter stalks. Young
asparagus plants are like baby chicks—it's nearly impossible to tell males from females. You don't have to pay
too much attention to sex if you order a batch of seeds.
You'll get a mixture of both. There are about 1,500
seeds to an ounce.

There are new varieties that are much better than the
older types; your seed catalog will help you choose

well. As yet, none of the varieties is 100 percent resistant to rust disease.

Beans
(PHASEOLUS VULGARIS)

With everyone health conscious today, beans are more popular than ever. People concerned about cholesterol can feel good about eating them. Nutritionists and health care specialists call beans high energy "seed foods." Nutritionists tell us that we need protein. People who cut down on meats find that beans are a good substitute.

Few garden vegetables yield so much. If picked frequently, beans will continue to produce over a long season. Snap beans are eaten fresh or cooked, pod and all. They can also be dried. Many bean varieties are for shelling and drying only. There are bush and pole (climbing) types. Your catalogs list all kinds: black beans, pink beans, black-eyed peas, chick-peas (garbanzos), fava beans, kidney beans, Royal Burgundy beans, lima, romano, pinto, great white northern, navy, French horticultural, and many more.

HISTORICAL FACTS: Some beans were known in the Old World before the time of Columbus. Archaeological discoveries dating back more than five millennia B.C. show beans to have been under at least incipient cultivation at that time.

STARTING SEED: The dwarf or bush varieties can be planted outdoors in rows 2 or 3 feet apart. Drop the beans (eyes down) about every 2 inches, cover with 1 inch of soil. If planted 3 inches apart, no thinning will be required. Do not plant until the soil is warm, or the beans will rot in the ground. After the ground is warm, you can plant them at intervals of 2 or 3 weeks if a constant supply of green beans is wanted. Beans are a warm-weather crop and will not germinate if the ground is cold.

POLE BEANS: If rabbits and other animals constantly bother your beans, grow them on poles or a trellis of some sort. Rough poles from wood work fine if set firmly into the ground. Plant about 5 or 6 bean seeds around each pole or stake and thin to the 3 strongest plants. You can tie the poles together at the top, tepee-fashion, or you can plant pole beans in a row along a fence or trellis, thinning to about 8 inches apart.

LIMA BEANS: A light sandy soil will produce the best set of lima bean pods, although limas will tolerate a workable clay soil. There are many good varieties; consult seed catalogs and your state agricultural college for those suitable to your area. You can tell a true lima bean seed by looking for lines running from the seed scar (hilum) to the dorsal suture (back) of it.

Lima beans are not as hardy as snap beans and shouldn't be planted too early. Plant them 1 inch deep, 3 beans to every 15 inches of row, in rows 3 feet apart if machine cultivator is used to work them, or 2 feet if hoed by hand. Make sure you place the eyes downward as it makes a difference in yield for all beans. Thin to 8 to 12 inches apart.

Don't crowd lima beans—they like plenty of room for extra large yields. Your seed sowing efforts will be lost if you cultivate too late. Stirring the soil will cause the buds and blossoms to drop. Bud drop may also be caused by hot, dry weather, over-feeding, cloudy weather, or wet weather. After your plants are up, mulch them with grass clippings, old newspapers, wood chips, or other mulch material to prevent dropping of flowers.

FAVA: Bean lovers are in for a real treat if they are willing to try a few fava or broad beans, sometimes called horse beans—a real misnomer. Fava plants are upright and contain 6 or 8 flat oblong beans in each 7-inch pod. Fava beans can be eaten fresh or as a winter shell bean with an unusually good flavor. Plant seed early in spring, as soon as soil can be worked since they do not like hot weather. Set seed about 8 inches apart in rows 3 feet apart. It takes 80 to 85 days for a crop to mature.

Dried beans for home use are grown in much the same way as garden beans except that the beans are allowed to ripen fully. Shell out the beans, dry thoroughly in a warm place, and then treat for weevils by placing the seeds in an oven at about 130 degrees F. for 30 minutes.

Bean weevils can ruin a jar of dry or shell beans needed for food or for seed, making them unfit for both. When beans are hulled and stored they may already be infested with the small white grubs. When you store them in a warm place the grubs mature and eat their way out of the dry beans, leaving small holes in the bean. When you eat fresh green beans from the garden you unknowingly eat the tiny eggs of the grubs. To avoid a weevil infestation in stored beans, here are three options:

1. Store beans in cans in an unheated outbuilding or porch (beans won't freeze).
2. Drop the beans in boiling water for 1 minute and then spread them out to dry. Do *not* use this method with beans to be used as seed.
3. Heat the beans in a shallow open container in the oven for 30 minutes at 130 degrees F. Seeds can be heated to a temperature of from 130 to 145 degrees F. without affecting their germination. A temperature of 135 degrees F. for 1 hour will kill almost any type of weevil that may be encountered. When heating the seed, spread it thinly so that the interior of each will reach the proper temperature.

Note: After the seed has been treated it is possible for it to become reinfested with weevils if it is not stored properly. Place it in glass jars or plastic bags that are tightly sealed.

Beets

(BETA VULGARIS)

Beets are easy to grow, yield heavily, and are rich in iron and vitamins, especially when the tops are included for greens. This is a "double-header" vegetable in that both the fleshy roots and leaves are edible.

HISTORICAL FACTS: The modern beet is a descendant of the wild beet of southern Europe whose leaves alone were consumed as a potherb in pre-Christian times.

STARTING SEED: Beets are so hardy the seed can be sown in the ground very early. Sow the seed in rows 14 to 18 inches apart, dropping 1 or 2 seeds to 1 inch of row. Cover with a half inch of soil. Don't plant too thickly—each "seed cluster" has 1 to 4 seeds in it. When plants are quite small, thin to 4 or 5 plants per 1 foot of row. A second planting in early July will give you tender beets for all use and winter storing. If you want to raise beets for greens only, just sow the seed thickly in broad rows 1 foot apart.

If you really want a good beet, try the Cylindra. It's cylindrical, dark red, 8 inches long, 1¾ inch across (the size of a large banana). And what tenderness! Sow the seed quite thickly, then thin some out for greens and let the bottoms of others grow. Sometimes they rise out of the ground. When you cook them with skins on the skins slide right off, like a banana peel. Cylindra matures in 55 days. Burpee Seed Company, Warminster, PA 18974, sells the seed.

Broccoli

(BRASSICA OLERACEA BOTRYTIS)

Broccoli

All members of the *Brassica* tribe, including cabbage, cauliflower, brussels sprouts, savoy cabbage, kale, etc., are easy to grow. Unfortunately, President George Bush singled out broccoli as a hated vegetable, but fortunately many thought he didn't know what he was talking about. Broccoli, whose edible part is in its flower, is one of the prettiest vegetables you can grow, and healthful as well!

HISTORICAL FACTS: Broccoli comes to us from Italy, where they really grow big ones. It's a favored vegetable in diets recommended by the American Heart Association and other health organizations, probably because of its abundance of chlorophyll, which is potent in blocking cell mutations.

STARTING SEED: There are two types of broccoli you can sow: the cauliflower type and the green sprouting, or Calabrese, type. The green sprouting type is what gardeners commonly call broccoli. For early crops, sow an early variety indoors, around April 10 in northern states. Transplant into pots or plant packs and then to open ground in early May. For other areas, consult your state college for proper planting dates. Space the plants 2½ feet apart each way.

For later crops, sow late varieties in June or earlier in some areas. Sow in the rows where they will remain. Thin to 2 feet apart, using some extras for transplanting.

Study your seed catalog for varieties suited to your area.

Note: There is a new hybrid, or cross, between broccoli and cauliflower, called "Broccoflower," admired by many consumers. Seed is listed in many seed catalogs and culture is same as for broccoli or cauliflower. There is another cole crop called "Romanasco" also quite popular, and it is listed in most catalogs.

Brussels Sprouts
(BRASSICA OLERACEA GEMMIFERA)

If you ask health care people around the world why they recommend eating green vegetables like brussels sprouts, they will point to the health benefits. In tests, brussels sprouts detoxified one of the world's most virulent carcinogens, aflatoxin, a fungal mold linked to high rates of cancer.

HISTORICAL FACT: Belgium developed brussels sprouts from a primitive relative, kale.

STARTING SEED: Brussels sprouts are not as easy to grow as cabbage, but they will be productive if plants are started early indoors or in a hotbed. Jade Cross is a good hybrid, but there are varieties for every area. When plants are 3 inches or so, transplant them into packs and let them grow to 5 or 6 inches. Then set them out in the garden, 2 feet apart in rows 3 feet apart. The largest sprouts are produced on the bottom of the plants and should be picked off and eaten as they mature; then the plants will continue to produce more sprouts up the stem until stopped by freezing weather. If you happen to grow more plants than you can use before heavy frost, take up the plants with some soil on the roots and stand them together in a cool cellar or garage where they will not freeze hard. Earth can be packed around the roots to keep the plants fresh so the sprouts will be crisp and tender.

Cabbage
(BRASSICA OLERACEA)

Cabbage has an ancient and esteemed place in diets and medical folklore.

HISTORICAL FACTS: A sixteenth-century historian wrote: "The old Romans having expelled physicians out of their commonwealth, did for many years maintain their health by the use of cabbages, taken for every disease." Interestingly, modern nutritionists are recommending cabbage and its relatives as highly beneficial in the diet.

STARTING SEED: There are early, midseason, and late cabbage varieties. All are easy to grow. Study your seed catalog and select disease resistant varieties to avoid yellows, a fungus that causes yellowing and dwarfing. Some yellows-resistant varieties are Golden Acre, Marion Market, Jersy Queen, Copenhagen, and Improved Wisconsin. There are others, depending on what varieties are best suited to your area.

Start your plants indoors or sow seed directly outdoors. Plants should stand 20 inches apart in rows 2½ to 3 feet apart. Early cabbage can be planted in May in the north, and late types can be set out in July. Your seed catalog or state college will recommend varieties and tell you the best time for sowing outdoors in your vicinity. Cabbage's only requirements are ample moisture and plant food, plus a nonacid soil. When ordering seed don't overlook savoy cabbage, one with a curled or savoyed head. Many folks prefer it for coleslaw and salads. And don't forget the redheads, excellent for salads, pickling, or coleslaw. Red cabbage contains over 30 times as much vitamin A as white cabbage. Here's a kitchen tip for people who object to cabbage, broccoli, or brussels sprouts because of the cooking odor. To eliminate odor, place a heel of bread on top of the vegetable, then put the lid on and *voilà*—no odor! Chinese cabbage (*Brassica rapa pekinensis*), called celery cabbage, is perhaps not a real cabbage but might be worth a try if you have a rich soil and plenty of water.

Carrot
(DAUCUS CAROTA)

Carrots

Carrots are called "Garden Gold" because they are so healthful to eat. Today's selection is the best ever and no garden should be without carrots. It's a cool-season vegetable best adapted to regions with long periods of mild weather that are free from extremes of temperature. Prolonged hot weather may retard growth, depress yield, and cause strong flavor.

HISTORICAL FACTS: The carrot is believed to have originated in Afghanistan. When carrots were first brought to England from Holland, stylish ladies used the feathery leaves to decorate their hair. At one time the carrot was chopped, dried, and used as a coffee substitute.

STARTING SEED: Carrot seed is slow to germinate and can be sown from late spring until late June. In dry weather, gently sprinkle the rows in the evening for a couple of weeks to insure quick "come up" and a good stand.

Make successive sowings every 2 or 3 weeks if you want a continous supply of tender young carrots throughout the season. Do not cover with more than a ¼inch of soil. Prevent a crust from forming by gently breaking the soil with a rake a few days after sowing. Sow a little radish seed with the carrots to mark the rows for cultivating and to help break the crust.

Thinning: Thin the early varieties to 2 inches and the large later varieties to 3 or 4 inches. If grown on a loose soil such as muck or sand, leave them thicker than on a heavy soil. Thin carrots just as soon as they come up or they will compete with each other for water and nutrients. However, if you want young tender carrots for table use in fall or winter, sow the seed thinly in mid-July and do not thin. You will get small, finger-size carrots that are excellent raw or cooked. Keep weeds down, as carrots will compete with them.

Cauliflower
(BRASSICA OLERACEA BOTRYTIS)

This is a variety of cabbage in which the head consists of the condensed and thickened flower clusters instead of the leaves. Mark Twain once said, "Training is everything. The peach was once a bitter almond, a cauliflower is nothing but cabbage with a college education."

HISTORICAL FACTS: The oldest records to mention cauliflower date back to the sixth century B.C. It was found on the London vegetable market as early as 1619 and has been grown in America for about 200 years. Like broccoli, cauliflower did not become popular in the United States until the past 40 years or so.

STARTING SEED: For early crops, sow seeds indoors in March (in the north) and set plants out 18 to 24 inches apart in rows 3 feet apart. In some areas cauliflower is hard to raise for an early crop as it does not head well during the hot summer months. You may have better luck sowing seed outdoors in late May and transplanting in June or July so the crop will head in September or October if these months are relatively frost free. It is very important that young plants not be checked in growth at any time. They must be kept growing steadily from the time seed is up or heads will be small and poor. Sometimes plants will start heading when only 2 inches tall. This is due to hot weather, regardless of soil moisture. Cauliflower likes the cool, moist months of fall; however, it cannot stand frost.

Celeriac
(APIUM GRAVEOLENS)

Celeriac is called "turnip root" or "knob" celery. It's not a very popular vegetable but is raised in the same manner as celery (see Celery). An 80-cent packet of seed started indoors might introduce you to a brand-new vegetable.

Celery
(APIUM GRAVEOLENS)

Celery

It isn't generally known that celery can be grown in most home gardens.

HISTORICAL FACT: As far as we know, it originated in the Mediterranean area.

STARTING SEED: Start seed in a Peat-Lite–type mix indoors in a window box or in cold frames. Cover the seed very lightly, if at all, and keep it moist and cool. To raise celery plants in the open ground, sow as early as the land can be worked. A fine soil is needed, well fertilized and if possible, fertilized with well-rotted manure. As it requires about 3 weeks for the plants to come up, scatter a little radish seed with the celery to mark the rows for cultivation and hasten germination.

Chard, Swiss
(BETA VULGARIS CICLA)

Swiss chard is unknown to many, but is one of the easiest vegetables to grow. You might say it is a beet grown for its leaves. It can withstand hot and cold weather and produces all season. There is a brilliantly colored red variety called rhubarb chard.

HISTORICAL FACT: Its origins are uncertain, but some references credit it to European countries.

STARTING SEED: Swiss chard is raised the same way as ordinary garden beets except that the rows should be 18 to 24 inches apart and the plants thinned to 8 inches apart. This can be done by first thinning to 4 inches and pulling out every other plant for use when they are 10 to 12 inches high.

Chicory
(CICHORIUM INTYBUS)

Chicory and endive (*C. endivia*) are closely related and belong to the same family as lettuce and dandelion. The terms chicory and endive are frequently interchanged because a forced type of chicory (witloof) has been erroneously named "French endive." Chicory is also known as succory. In the United States it is grown principally as a salad crop and for its roots, which when dried and ground serve as an adulterant for coffee.

HISTORICAL FACT: It is said to have originated in the Mediterranean area.

STARTING SEED: Start seed 110 to 130 days before the average date of killing frosts in the fall. Planting too early results in plants going to seed, or in oversized, multiple-hearted roots.

Chives
(ALLIUM SCHOENOPRASUM)

Chives grow successfully indoors and outdoors.

HISTORICAL FACT: Some researchers claim that chives came from Europe.

STARTING SEED: Chives come up year after year and are exceedingly easy to grow. Start seed indoors in pots around March 1 and grow it in a sunny window. You can transplant clumps outdoors in pots or directly into the garden. You can bring a clump inside from the outdoors in fall and pot it, or start seed indoors and grow it in a window box or pots yearlong.

Corn
(Z E A   M A Y S)

You can't beat home-grown corn for freshness and taste. Hybridizers have given us the best varieties ever. Corn is a warm-weather crop so try to get the seed in the ground as soon as possible so it can grow through the hot summer weather. See also Popcorn.

HISTORICAL FACT: Corn originated in the Americas, probably in Central America.

STARTING SEED: Sow seed in blocks of at least 3 rows side by side (rather than in a single row) to ensure pollination and development of a full set of kernels. Space the rows 2 to 3 feet apart and drop the seed 4 to 5 inches apart for later thinning to 8 to 10 inches apart for the early varieties, and 12 to 18 inches apart for the later kinds. To grow corn in hills or groups, use 5 or 6 seeds per hill 2 to 3 feet apart. Hills are groups of seeds planted together, not mounds of soil. Thin to 3 plants of early kinds and 2 of later varieties.

Seedsmen will tell you that even on high germination seed you can expect a loss of about 15 percent on the final stand. Just what happens to this 15 percent no one knows. Make successive plantings about 10 days apart to enjoy a long season of sweet corn. Or try planting an early, midseason, and late variety at the same time, and your corn won't mature all at once. An additional planting of a midseason variety about a month later will yield fine corn in early fall.

Note: Usually early corn is more wormy than late corn, especially in areas where there is only one brood of corn borer. The moth is done laying eggs by the time much of the late corn comes along.

Seed catalogs are singing the praises of new sweet corn varieties that hold their sweetness longer than standard corn varieties. Within a day of picking, the conversion of sugar to starch makes ears taste flat and starchy. The standard sweet corns lose sweetness and quality if not cooled below 50 degrees as soon as possible. Enhanced corn has a higher initial sugar content than standard corn, so it stays sweet longer. The new "sweet sweet" corn varieties have somewhat technical names. In the catalogs you'll see terms like Supersweet, Sugary Enchanced, EH (Everlasting Heritage), Extra-Sweet Hybrid, etc., but before you order seed for your garden, consult with your seedsman. Don't go overboard and dump the standard varieties—you may be disappointed. We haven't given up our older types because, frankly, in spite of all the genetic engineering that's gone into corn, some old varieties are difficult to beat. There's a good selection today because some hybrid sweet corn has rapidly replaced many open-pollinated varieties in home gardens. However, that doesn't mean a hybrid is superior because it happens to be a hybrid. Try growing an early, midseason, and late variety. Study catalogs for recommended varieties for your area.

Cucumber
(C U C U M I S   S A T I V U S)

Cucumbers are a warm season crop and should be planted when all danger of frost has passed. There are many fine varieties to select from. The long varieties are used primarily for slicing, and are ready in 52 to 65 days. Varieties that are blunt-ended when small are preferred for pickles. There are many on the market ideal for bread-and-butter pickles, pickle chunks, and pickle slices. You should get a good crop of pickles in about 45 days.

STARTING SEED: Cucumbers can be raised in unevenly spaced rows or in hills. Avoid planting until the night temperatures are above 40 degrees or seed will rot.

You can grow cucumbers in barrels, on trellises, or anyplace they can climb, such as porch railings. If you want a cucumber that doesn't talk back to you, grow the burpless variety. This cuke is slender, often crooked (it can grow from 12 to 24 inches long), easy to grow, and easy to eat.

Cucumbers do not cross with muskmelons, watermelons, pumpkins, or squash as many believe. Different cucumber varieties will cross-pollinate, however. This does not affect the edible portion. If you saved seeds from cross-pollinated plants, next year's crop will be a mixture.

Eggplant
(SOLANUM MELONGENA)

Eggplants used to be difficult to grow, but with the new varieties they are of the same culture as peppers. Select the early varieties for cultivation in northern areas. The number of days from setting-out to harvest can vary from 52 to 80 days, depending on the variety. They will mature quicker if you use black plastic mulch.

HISTORICAL FACTS: Eggplant is believed to have originated in northern India. Apparently the species was spread to Europe and Arabic peoples during the Dark Ages.

STARTING SEED: Seed should be started indoors in a temperature between 70 and 90 degrees F. Seed will not come up if the temperature is lower. When seedlings are 2 inches high, transplant singly into pots. Eggplants do not transplant easily. It takes about 8 or 9 weeks to grow plants to proper size for setting out. A patch of six plants will produce all the fruits that an average family of five will need. Set plants 24 to 30 inches apart. Make sure you wash your hands with soap and water before handling the seedlings if you use tobacco in any form to avoid spreading of tobacco mosaic disease. (This applies to all members of the Solanaceae family—tomatoes, potatoes, petunias, peppers, etc.)

Endive
(CICHORIUM ENDIVIA)

Finely curled or fringed-leaved varieties of endive are grown as a salad crop. Broad-leaved varieties are grown as a late fall and winter crop in the south and shipped in a green or partly blanched condition to northern markets and called escarole, which is similar in culture to lettuce.

HISTORICAL FACT: This species came from the eastern Mediterranean area and was cultivated by ancient Egyptians.

STARTING SEED: Sow seed in June or July. For

early use, plant outdoors as soon as possible. Seed is sown shallow, ⅛ inch apart in rows ¼ inch deep in rows 18 to 24 inches apart. Thin plants to 8 to 12 inches apart.

Fennel
(FOENICULUM OFFICINALIS)

Bulb fennel, also known as finocchio, is best grown as a spring or fall crop as it tends to develop seed stalks in hot weather. The fresh licorice-like flavor gives a pleasant taste, and is good in salads.

HISTORICAL FACT: A native of Europe.

STARTING SEED: Plant outside in early May for a spring crop and in late June or July for fall use. When bulbs begin to form, draw earth up to cover and blanch them.

Gourds
(CUCURBITA)

The hard-shelled fruits commonly known as gourds are not edible but are in big demand by interior decorators. Gourds are of two general types: highly colored small sorts (spoon, pear, apple, orange, egg, warted, etc.) in solid orange, yellow, green, and white, and in stripes and bicolors, and the large sorts (calabash, dipper, Hercules' Club, etc.), often used as containers and utensils.

HISTORICAL FACT: Believed to have originated in the Mediterranean or Middle East.

STARTING SEED: You can start plants from seed planted in May and temporarily grow in pots; when warm weather arrives set plants outdoors to grow on a fence, wire trellis, screen, etc., or let them ramble. If weather is warm, sow seed outdoors in hills or clusters, 4 feet apart each way. Gourds will not stand much frost.

Kale
(BRASSICA OLERACEA ACEPHALA)

Kale is a type of cabbage and is an excellent green for late fall. Also called borecole, this cabbage does not form a head. It is good for winter and early spring use, ideal for garnishing, and can even be used in flower arrangements. Years ago it was much more popular than now, but it is making a comeback, thanks to food nutritionists.

HISTORICAL FACTS: The Greeks grew kale, and Roman gardeners developed a number of varieties. It was brought to America in 1540 by the French explorer

Jacques Cartier, who planted both kale and cabbage along the St. Lawrence to provide food for his men through the winter. Chinese cabbage, now familiar in American markets, is a form of kale. It has been grown in China for 2,000 years.

Note: Ornamental kale, a decorative kale that is red, pink, or white, has reached the flower garden as a handsome ornamental plant. Flowering kale and flowering cabbage are both ornamental *and* edible (see Chapter 3, Annuals). They take about the same care as all the *Brassicas.*

STARTING SEED: Kale is closely related to broccoli, cabbage, and other *Brassicas.* Seed-starting directions are the same as for those relatives.

Kohlrabi
(BRASSICA OLERACEA CAULORAPA)

Kohlrabi is a forgotten vegetable that needs rediscovery. This member of the cabbage family produces a swelled stem that is edible. Its interior is white, its exterior light green. It's easy to grow and can be eaten raw or boiled. Early White Vienna and Grand Duke are the most important varieties grown.

STARTING SEED: Sow seed outdoors at any time from May to July in rows 18 inches to 2 feet apart. Or, you can start seed early in hotbeds and set plants out like early cabbage. Young plants should be transplanted or thinned to stand about 6 inches apart in the row. Kohlrabi is at its best when grown in cool days of spring. However, it is also excellent as a fall crop. Use it while it is young and tender, not larger than a baseball.

Lettuce
(LACTUCA SATIVA)

There is no question that lettuce is the most popular salad plant. Leaf lettuce is the most popular with home gardeners because it's so easy to grow. Good leaf varieties are Salad Bowl and Black-Seeded Simpson. Study your seed catalog for varieties that are "slow to bolt"—that is, slow to go to seed in the heat of summer. We like Buttercrunch, a semihead type.

HISTORICAL FACT: According to early writings, lettuce was served at the tables of the Persian kings of the sixth century B.C.

STARTING SEED: Sow the seed of leaf lettuce outdoors any time from early spring until July, making several plantings for a continuous supply. Plant in rows about 2 feet apart, and cover seed very lightly. Some gardeners thin the plants, using the thinnings for salad—a great idea. You can cut the lettuce top close to the soil level and new growth will appear.

If you have had trouble getting seed to germinate in hot weather, try putting it in the refrigerator prior to planting. This treatment makes the seed come up faster. Put the seed in a shallow dish (with no water), place it in the refrigerator for 24 hours; then sow. Another trick is to mix Bibb lettuce seed with sand; in February when there's a thaw, scatter the seed on the ground and forget it. In May, you should have the privilege of harvesting some fresh early lettuce.

Mushrooms
(AGARICUS CAMPESTRIS)

It's possible to raise edible mushrooms in the basement of your home during fall and winter months, but don't expect to get rich making money in the cellar. The Federal Trade Commission told us that in one year the public paid one company $328,000 for mushroom kits, and were only able to sell $5,324 worth of mushrooms back to the company. However, don't let this discourage you from trying to grow a few mushrooms in the cellar. Commercially prepared mushroom trays are viable and they are ready to bear a crop as soon as they're given the right conditions.

STARTING SEED: Mushrooms do not produce

seed, but spores. You can buy mushroom "spawn" in brick form. Scatter the spores or spawn over specially prepared trays containing rotted compost or horse manure situated in a dark room or cellar. It takes about 3 weeks to get mushrooms the size of pinheads. These increase in size daily until mature. The mushrooms grow in "flushes"—that is, they pop up all over the place.

The most common failure with mushrooms comes from high temperatures. *If temperatures are over 75 degrees F. for as much as a day, failure will result.* If the air temperature drops below 50 degrees F. the crop will be delayed, if not killed. Mushrooms need temperatures between 52 and 65 degrees F., and they need darkness since they are a fleshy fungus with no chlorophyll. Mushrooms do not make their own food, as do green plants.

Muskmelons
(CUCUMIS MELO)

There's no reason why you can't grow sweet muskmelons right in your own backyard. Muskmelons are so named because of the delightful odor of the ripe fruits, musk being a Persian word for a kind of perfume. The varieties known as cantaloupe, honeydew, casaba, and Persian melons are all muskmelons. All cantaloupes are muskmelons but many varieties and types of muskmelons are not cantaloupes, thus our use of the broader term.

HISTORICAL FACTS: The muskmelon is native to Persia (Iran) and adjacent areas. The oldest record of muskmelon is an Egyptian painting of 2400 B.C. Columbus carried muskmelon seed on his second voyage to the New World and had them planted on Isabella Island in 1494. This was undoubtedly their first culture in the New World.

STARTING SEED: Muskmelons (and most melons) like a well-drained soil and dislike "wet feet." They need a long growing season and hot, dry weather. Melons are likely to be of inferior quality in cool, cloudy seasons. For best results start them indoors in a light, rich, sterilized soil. Start them in peat pots or Jiffy pellets, 2 or 3 seeds per pot, and thin to 1 or 2 strong plants. Be sure to keep the soil very warm—70 to 80 degrees both *day and night* during germination. The plants will be ready for setting out in 3 or 4 weeks.

You can also plant them outdoors using black plastic mulch, which heats the soil, conserves moisture, and cuts down on weeds, hastening growth. Cut holes in the mulch and put 10 seeds in each hill. After the true leaves appear, thin the plants to 4 seedlings per hill. If you plant the seed in rows, sow 3 or 4 seeds per foot and thin to 12 to 15 inches apart.

Mustard Greens
(B R A S S I C A   J U N C E A)

If you want easy-to-grow, ideal greens, try the mustard

plant. Chances are it came from China, where it is called bok choy.

STARTING SEED: Sow early in spring; broadcast or plant 2 or 3 inches apart. Make successive plantings. For fall use, plant seed in August.

Try Burpee's Fordhook Fancy for green leaves that curve backward like ostrich plumes. Other varieties include Green Wave, and Florida Broadleaf from Stokes, and Tendergreens and Savanna Hybrid from Park Seed.

Okra
(HIBISCUS ESCULENTUS)

Either you like okra (also known as gumbo) or you don't. Those who don't like it probably never tried it. Southerners rely on it because, like butter beans and cowpeas, it will continue to bear in spite of summer heat. You can grow okra as far north as New York State. It likes full sun.

HISTORICAL FACTS: Okra is believed to have originated in northeastern Africa. It was used in Egypt for centuries and spread to the Far East.

STARTING SEED: Soak seeds in warm water for 12 hours prior to planting. Plant in rows 2½ to 3 feet apart; then thin plants to 1 foot apart.

Onion

(ALLIUM CEPA)

Onion in one or more of its many forms is found in practically every home garden. Onions are grown from seed, sets (bulblets), or plants, depending on the purpose and the variety.

HISTORICAL FACTS: In ancient cultures no foods were as esteemed for their health (and magic) qualities as garlic and its cousin, onion—both members of the Allium family. These vegetables, highly popular today, are as old as agriculture itself. Evidence of their use as food, in religious rites, and in healing shows up in tombs in ancient Sumeria (4000 B.C.). Bulbs are pictured on the walls of tombs in ancient Egypt (3200 B.C.) and in the ruins of Pompeii and Herculaneum (100 A.D.). Today, all good cooks use onions and garlic in meals.

STARTING SEED: To start onions from seed, sow thickly in rows 2 inches apart (drop 8 seeds per inch to allow for maggot damage) and cover them with about $\frac{1}{2}$ inch of soil. Thin out to 1 or 1½ inches apart for small green onions and 3 or 4 inches for large mature bulbs. (The thinnings can be used for green onions or boiling onions.)

Both early green bunching onions and large dry onions are very easily started from sets, which are small onion bulbs ½ to ¾ inches across and produced from seed the previous year. Sets should be planted early in the spring, about 3 inches apart, in rows 18 to 20 inches apart. If you want small early onions, plant more thickly. We dig a trench and put the onions in it, close enough so they touch one another. Cover sets completely with soil and pull them for green onions in a few weeks, or thin and let them mature until July into large onions. Some gardeners make successive plantings of sets for green onions during the spring and early summer. Although these plants can be allowed to mature to dry bulbs, they are not as good for storage as those grown from seed or plants.

If you like the big "hamburger" onions (Bermuda and Spanish types), set out the seedling onion plants early in spring. These take a long growing season so they are started in the South where the seeds can be sown early. You buy them in bunches ready to plant. The large sweet onions indigenous to certain areas of the country (Vidalia from Georgia, Walla Walla from Washington State, Texas Sweet) are adapted to those areas specifically because of soil and climate. They never taste the same when grown outside their own territory.

Multiplier onions are hardy perennials planted in the fall, which provide early spring eating. More common than multipliers is the perennial or "tree" or "top" onion (Egyptian), a common winter onion on which clusters of small onions (bulblets) are produced on top of the onion stalk and which can be planted for green onions.

Shallots, related to onions, seldom produce seeds, so plant small bulbs or bulblets in spring and harvest around August. Leeks look like green onions but do not form bulbs. They are grown from seed sown 2 inches deep in a trench. Thin to 3 inches apart in a row. Seed can be sown indoors in March and plants set in the garden in April for an early crop.

Garlic has become one of the most popular members of the onion family. Previously the butt of jokes, it is now in such big demand that garlic rustlers steal the mature cloves from the fields in California. Historically, garlic was thought of as a body strengthener. Builders of the Great Pyramid at Giza ate garlic to build muscle and vigor. An Egyptian medical papyrus dating from about 1500 B.C. listed twenty-two garlic prescriptions. Today, no serious American cook would be without garlic.

Garlic plants do not readily produce seeds. Both commercially and in the home garden, cloves (divisions of the bulb) are used for reproduction. Plant cloves right side up, about 1 inch deep and 4 inches apart in September or October. By the following August, bulbs will be ready to harvest. They must be dried (cured) on racks in a dry, airy place. Folks who want a mild garlic flavor can pot up two or three cloves in a pot, then snip off some of the green shoots as they grow.

Parsley

(PETROSELINUM CRISPUM)

Parsley is one of the best "herbs" or vegetables you can grow. It'll do well in any good garden soil and will also do well in partial shade. Refer to catalogs for best varieties of extra fine curled leaves and plain leaves. You might like the parsnip-rooted parsley. Roots are used, boiled and served like parsnips. The flat-leaved "celery" parsley is preferred by many cooks. We prefer curled leaves.

HISTORICAL FACTS: The Romans used to put a sprig of parsley on the brow of people who were to be buried. This plant is believed to have originated somewhere in the Mediterranean.

STARTING SEED: Parsley has a "growth inhibitor" on the seed coat, delaying germination. You can bypass this by drenching the seed in very warm water (120 degrees. F.) for 10 minutes. Some people put seed in water and freeze it for 24 hours before planting. Germination is slow. Start seed indoors in peat pots or small flats and transplant while young. Remember: Parsley has a tap root (instead of fibrous roots), so be sure to transplant them directly in the garden when about an inch tall. You can mix a few radish seeds with it, cover with ½ inch of soil, and keep moist until germination starts.

Parsnip
(PASTINACA SATIVA)

Here is welcome addition to the list of so-called winter vegetables. Anyone who's had french-fried parsnips will agree this fine vegetable should be in every home garden.

HISTORICAL FACT: This relative of the carrot is native to the Mediterranean area.

STARTING SEED: Parsnips should be grown in a rich, humusy soil. Sow seed in April or May directly in the ground. Drop 3 or 4 seeds to the inch in rows 24 to 30 inches apart. Do not cover seed too deeply as it has little "pushing" power and will not come up. A ¼-inch covering is plenty, or you can sprinkle seed lightly with sand or vermiculite. Deep covering produces more failures with parsnips than any other cause. Sow radish seed with parsnip to break the crust. When plants are small, thin them to 3 inches apart.

Leave parsnips in the ground all winter for an early spring harvest. Put a light mulch of hay or straw over the row and they'll keep wonderfully.

Pea
(PISUM)

Peas

There is a wonderful selection of peas for the home garden. The newer edible podded peas, including Sugar Snap, Sugar Mel, Sugar Ann, and Snow Peas, have great flavor and there's no waste as the pods are tender if picked at the right time. There are dwarf bush types as well as long vined ones.

HISTORICAL FACTS: Medieval Europeans relied on peas as a staple food to stave off famines and see them through wars. Until the seventeen century, peas were used only in dried form. But once the flavor was discovered, fresh green peas became intensely fashionable among royal ladies of France.

STARTING SEED: Peas are a cool-season crop. In fact, light freezing in the spring will not harm the vines. It's best to sow early, medium, and late varieties all at the same time so as to have a succession of tasty meals. Or you can make a second sowing about 3 weeks after the first. Keep in mind that peas sown in summer rarely succeed on account of hot dry weather. However,

Wando is a variety that tolerates hot weather. We have sown Wando as late as July 15 and still had good tender peas. Some gardeners train their vines on a trellis, others let them ramble. And one more point, inoculate the pea seed with a bacterial preparation that comes with the seed. This inoculant takes nitrogen from the air and converts it into plant food for peas.

Peanuts
(ARACHIS HYPOGAEA)

Although a long season crop, peanuts can be successfully grown in regions as far north as New York State. The pods and nuts are formed underground. After the flowers are pollinated, the short stalks which bear them become elongated and bend down and push the flower into the soil where it develops into a pod of peanuts. Many plant lovers sow the seed in hanging baskets, as they make quite a conversation piece.

HISTORICAL FACTS: Peanuts were grown by South American Indians more than 1,000 years ago and came to the southern U.S. in the 1600s. They were unknown in the northern states until after the Civil War, but baseball made them famous.

After Union veterans changed into civilian clothes, baseball was a pursuit many turned to. Ball parks opened in towns and villages. Spectators needed a "pacifier" to chew on between cheers so they tried the delicious "groundnuts" being sold at the "gate." They thought of the groundnuts roasted over their campfires during lulls in the fighting. Pretty soon some entrepreneurs responded to the nostalgic yearnings of the ex-soldiers, and peddlers started carrying peanuts with their popcorn.

The first slaves were introduced into Virginia in 1619. During the eighteenth-and nineteenth-century years of the slave trade, peanuts were the accepted food for slave ships because they kept so well. Slaves liked peanuts so much, the story goes, that many of them hid peanuts in their hair for later planting. They called them "nguba"—the Bantu word for groundnut—and it was corrupted to "goober." Some southerners still call peanuts "goober peas"—one of the few words of African origin transferred to American English.

George Washington Carver, born of slave parents in 1854, worked his way through Iowa State College and became the foremost researcher of agricultural products, but specialized in peanuts. He gave humanity more than 300 products made from peanuts, including peanut butter.

STARTING SEED: An early frost will kill the plants, so seed should be sown (either in their hulls or shelled) as soon as frost danger is past. Shelled nuts can be placed 3 to 6 inches apart. If in the hulls, plant about 8 inches apart. Cover with 1½ inches of soil. Before frost in fall, dig or lift the entire vine and hang under an open shed to cure.

Pepper
(CAPSICUM FRUTESCENS)

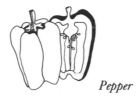

Pepper

Peppers are popular both raw and cooked. They need more heat than tomatoes and a longer growing season. Study seed catalogs and order varieties to suit your area, otherwise you're apt to get "all bush and no fruit."

HISTORICAL FACTS: Garden peppers both hot and mild have been an archaeological puzzle for years. Fragments have been recorded in Mexican caves dating back to around 7000 B.C. In Greco-Roman medicine every doctor advocated "building a fire in your stomach" as a remedy for colds. Hot peppers are still recommended by many health proponents. It is claimed that Mexicans and others who eat "hot" food have less respiratory trouble. The heat producer is capsaicin (pronounced "cap-SAY-uh-sin").

STARTING SEED: Start your seed early indoors (February or March) in seed flats filled with a Peat-Lite–type mix (vermiculite, sand and peat mixture, perlite, sphagnum are all good). Sow the seed lightly and cover with a fine sifting of peat or vermiculite. Place the flat in a shallow pan of water and allow water to come up from below. Put a pane of glass or plastic over the box until seed starts to sprout. Keep germinating temperature between 70 and 80 degrees or seed will be slow to germinate or may rot. After seeds sprout remove glass and put the box or flat in a bright window. Peppers are also sold already started in containers. Buy from a dependable garden store so you will get the right variety. Transplant 1 foot apart in rows 2 feet apart in loose soil. Use paper collars to protect plants from cut worms. *Note*: A black plastic mulch holds the heat in the soil and hastens growth. It's worth the effort. All hot peppers are edible, including the ornamental Christmas pepper often used as a house plant. You start these the same as you do regular peppers.

Popcorn

Popcorn, and various novelty corns, such as Indian corn and other ornamental corns, require the same care as sweet corn.

STARTING SEED: Use the same directions as for sweet corn.

Note: Sweet corn should not be planted next to popcorn or ornamental corn, if both have the same ripening date. If you plant sweet corn next to ornamental corn, be sure to use an early or midseason sweet corn to avoid getting sweet corn ears with purple, orange, or yellow kernels. Since ornamental corn is late, it won't shed pollen at the same time as the early corn. So if you're going to plant ornamental corn along with edible corn, be sure to select an early-maturing variety of sweet corn.

Potato
(SOLANUM TUBEROSUM)

Many gardeners are yearning for a good eating potato since store spuds often lack quality. Considering the space potato plants need, we don't recommend growing your own in a small garden, especially if you live in an area where you can buy good potatoes.

HISTORICAL FACTS: No doubt about it, the popular potato is a native of the Andes in South America. It was unknown in North America before the Spaniards came to the New World. The Spanish called it *batata* and it made an official entry into what we now call the United States—shipped to the first Spanish colony founded in St. Augustine—in 1565. History books say that Sir Francis Drake took a supply of white potatoes with him and these were planted on Sir Walter Raleigh's estate in Ireland, thus starting the history of the so-called Irish potato. Few vegetables have as fascinating a history as the potato. Immigration of thousands of Irish citizens to the United States was initiated by the blight which killed the potato crop in 1845.

STARTING SEED: You can start potatoes from seed if you can find a seed house that sells it. The results are fascinating. The potatoes may be of different shapes and sizes, because the potato flowers may have been pollinated by an unknown variety. Most gardeners use small tubers (about 1¼ to 2 ounces.) or large tubers cut in pieces (called seed pieces). If you use cut-up tubers, you must be sure you have an eye on each piece. The eye is the indentation where the sprout originates.

Most seed firms now sell eyes because they are less expensive to ship. Each eye will have some flesh around it to feed the young sprouts as they take root. When buying tubers, be sure they are certified seed stock if you want a known variety, free from diseases.

NOTE: Potatoes produce tiny tomatolike fruits on top of the mature plant. These are the potato seed, developed from the flowers. When small, these structures look like small tomatoes, and some people call them "potato balls" or "potato apples." They are nothing but seed pods of potatoes and NOT EDIBLE; they can be toxic. Do not bother planting seed from them. Some people erroneously think these small balls are the result of the potato crossing with a tomato.

Potato, Sweet
(IPOMOEA BATATAS)

The yam is a large starchy tuber grown in tropical areas of the world. True yams are not considered edible by modern man unless he is faced with starvation. Those "yams" you see in the stores are sweet potatoes and they can be grown any place where there is a frost-free period of 150 days.

HISTORICAL FACT: They are native to Africa.

STARTING SEED: "Seed" from sweet potatoes are eyes or buds. They produce many eyes—as many as 50 to a medium-sized potato. Buy the sweet potato vines already started and grow them with black plastic mulch to hold soil moisture, control weeds, and raise the soil temperature—the latter being very important in the production of sweet potatoes.

Pumpkins
(*See* SQUASH AND PUMPKINS)

Radish
(RAPHANUS SATIVIS)

Radish

Radishes are easy to grow and quick to mature. They grow best in cool weather and become hot tasting in hot weather. Small round varieties mature more quickly than long ones.

HISTORICAL FACT: Said to be native to China.

STARTING SEED: A simple packet of radish seed will sow 25 to 30 feet. Sow seed in rows and cover ¼ inch. Thin plants to about ½ inch apart. Make additional sowings every few weeks for continuous supply, except during hot, dry weather, when they don't do well. Best radishes are those raised in greenhouses or hotbeds as they are not as sharp tasting as those grown outside. A few radish seeds mixed in at planting time with such vegetables as carrots, parsley, and parsnips will mark the rows for the slower-growing crops and help break the surface crust for fine seed.

Rhubarb
(RHEUM RHAPONTICUM)

A good patch of rhubarb or "pieplant" will last 25 years or more. One of the few vegetables in which the stem is used as food. It is treated like fruit.

HISTORICAL FACTS: Native to Asia Minor. Chinese rhubarb was used as medicine as early as 2700 B.C.

STARTING SEED: Starting plants from seed is not a reliable means. Divide roots from a neighbor's patch or buy started roots from a nursery.

Rutabaga
(B R A S S I C A   N A P O B R A S S I C A)

Rutabagas, or "Swede turnips," are becoming more popular with home gardeners. Rutabagas are similar to turnips except they have smooth instead of hairy leaves. They also have larger roots and need a month longer to mature.

HISTORICAL FACTS: Believed to have originated as a cross between a turnip and cabbage in Europe sometime during the Middle Ages. It appeared in literature first in 1620, and while more nutritious than turnips it is grown more extensively in Europe than America.

STARTING SEED: You can get a heavy crop by sowing the seed June 15 to July 1, in rows 2 feet apart. Rutabagas need a heavy soil for best growth. Thin to 1 foot apart. Dust the plants with wood ashes to check flea beetles.

They will stand considerable frost. After heavy frosts have come, lift them, top the plants, and store the roots in moist sand in a cool part of the cellar, or wax for storage.

The rutabaga is the only root crop we know of that is waxed to last longer in storage. Paraffin can be used, although produce companies use a special vegetable wax which is not conspicuous. For home use simply melt the paraffin, dip the rutabagas, and let them dry. Rutabagas retain their quality in storage better than turnips.

Troubles: Corky growth, due to excess nitrogen or hot weather, which also causes bitterness.

Salsify
(TRAGOPOGON PORRIFOLIUS)

Salsify, or "vegetable oyster," is one of the unsung vegetables. Long fleshy roots have an oysterlike flavor and are ideal in late fall, winter, or early spring. Flavor improves with frost, so the crop can be left in the ground all winter covered with straw.

HISTORICAL FACT: Native to the Mediterranean countries, where it can still be found growing wild.

STARTING SEED: Like carrots, salsify seeds need a loose, sandy soil and should be treated in the same manner.

Spinach
(SPINACIA OLERACEA)

Spinach is still a leading "greens," rich in iron, calcium, and Vitamin A. It's a quick-growing, hardy crop which thrives best in cool weather. It's often called "king of the vegetable greens" and one that "has it all."

HISTORICAL FACT: A native to Southwest Asia.

STARTING SEED: Plant as early in spring as possible in rows 14 to 18 inches apart, covering seed about ½ inch. Thin plants to 5 or 6 inches apart in the row. Successive plantings will give you a supply throughout the season. After the middle of May, use only long-standing varieties since others do not do well in hot weather. For fall use, sow in August, and to winter over, sow the seed about the first of September. Since spinach usually gets blighted in the fall, a blight resistant variety should be used for sowing after the middle of July.

Spinach, New Zealand
(TETRAGONIA EXPANSA)

The low-spreading "summer spinach," or New Zealand spinach, is not a true spinach. A native of Australia, New Zealand spinach has long been used as a substitute for regular spinach.

STARTING SEED: Seed has a hard seed coat. Soak in warm water for 24 hours or so before planting. Rows should be 3 feet apart, as the plants spread out nearly 2 feet each side of the row. Tender new leaves at the tips of the branches may be picked off as wanted in summer and fall. This spinach is killed by hard frost.

Squash and Pumpkins
(CUCURBITA)

No vegetable exceeds the squash in variety of form and color. Summer and winter squash have about the same culture as melons and cucumbers.

Winter Squash

HISTORICAL FACT: They were the staple diet of the ancient civilizations of the New World. Remains have been found in Mexico dating back as far as 5000 B.C.

STARTING SEED OF SUMMER SQUASH AND PUMPKINS: Sow the seed in "hills" (clusters), 3 or 4 feet apart. Plant 8 or 10 seeds in a hill and cover with 1 inch of soil. Later, thin plants to 3 in a hill. Cultivation should be shallow to avoid injuring roots. Will pumpkins and squash cross or mix in the garden? All the varieties within a species will mix or cross. So all varieties of *Curcurbita pepo* (summer squashes and most

Zucchini

pumpkins) will cross, but this is not a problem to the average gardener unless he saves his own seed. Pumpkins and squashes cannot be crossed with cucumbers, muskmelons, or watermelons, so you can't blame poor taste on cross pollination with these.

STARTING SEED OF WINTER SQUASH: Needs more space to grow than summer squash. Plant in rows 7 to 8 feet apart for smaller types as butternut, acorn, and buttercup, and in rows 9 feet apart for the larger types, such as Hubbard. Plant in hills 4 feet apart in the rows with 8 to 10 seeds to the hill. Then thin to 3 plants per hill after plants are up. The most popular winter squash is the acorn, or Table Queen.

Zucchini is a summer squash and should be treated as such.

Tomato

(L Y C O P E R S I C O N   E S C U L E N T U M)

The tomato is the number one vegetable. Even the hardpressed suburbanite saves a place in both garden and schedule to raise a few tomatoes. You don't need a big backyard to grow a big crop of tomatoes.

A friend plants six hybrid tomatoes and picks 4½ bushels each year. Our advice is to try three or four different kinds of red tomatoes—early, midseason, and late. Order resistant varieties. The catalog will mark them F (fusarium resistant), V (verticillium resistant), and N (nematode resistant). There is no such thing as a disease-free tomato—they all get some disease. Orange and yellow tomatoes are good eating and you might want to plant a few cherry tomatoes (such as Sweet 100 or Sweet Million). You might even want to select a few novelties such as Snow White (white when ripe), Evergreen (green when fully ripe), or even a blue tomato. Window-box gardeners have many dwarf hybrids to choose from.

HISTORICAL FACTS: The tomato is native to tropical America, in the Peru/Ecuador area. It was brought from Mexico to Europe in 1523. It was presented to the continent as the *pomme d'amour*, or "love apple."

STARTING SEED: There are early, midseason, and late tomatoes. If you live in a region where frosts come early in the fall, select an early-maturing variety. If you don't, you'll have green tomatoes at harvest time. Start seeds 6 to 8 weeks before you want to transplant outdoors. Seedlings can then be transplanted to individual pots. You can use peat pots or Jiffy pellets. These can be set in the garden without checking the growth, as the plants need not be removed from the pot. Pots will decay and furnish plant food as they break down in the soil. Or you can use ordinary clay pots, which can be used year after year. Many gardeners transplant seedlings to plant packs, then separate the transplants when it's time to plant them outdoors. Potted tomatoes may grow tall and have blossoms on at transplanting time, but don't worry—you can set them into the ground deeply and they'll form roots all the way up the stem. When the plant takes hold you'll see it practically jump. Some folks like to use a booster or transplanting solution of a high-analysis, water-soluble complete fertilizer at planting time to give the plant a quick send-off.

HORMONE SPRAYS: Unpollinated or incompletely pollinated tomato flowers often fail to set fruit and drop off the plants, especially in the early part of the season, due to cool nights (below 59 degrees F.) or short, cloudy days and lack of sunlight—all conditions unfavorable for pollination. "Blossomset" hormone sprays will ripen tomatoes 1 to 3 weeks earlier than usual. The blossom-set spray, available at garden supply stores, holds the fruit on the plants. The hormone chemical starts fruit development by chemical stimulation of the flowers. Many of the tomatoes will be seedless because the fruit is set by chemicals, not by pollen.

The spray comes in aerosol cans, or in liquid form ready for dilution. Spray the flower clusters when they are open or partly open. We spray the first cluster as soon as two or more blossoms are open, and make repeated sprayings weekly to set flowers that open later.

CHILLING THE SEEDLINGS: Another way to produce early fruit on tomato vines is to chill the tomato seedlings after the seed leaves, or cotyledons, unfold, when seedlings are about 1 to 1½ inches tall. You get remarkable benefits by chilling the seedlings 2 or 3 weeks at 50 to 55 degrees F. (night temperature). Chilling the young plants not only increases the flowers, but results in early yields. Chilled plants are stockier, have thicker stems, and a better chance of survival after transplanting. Also, flower numbers in the first and second clusters are more than doubled. Fruit clusters are larger and early yields may be greater. The flower number and the position of the first cluster are determined 4 to 6 weeks before the first flowers open. Flower formation occurs during the 2- or 3-week interval immediately following the expansion of the seed leaves (these are the first to show up), and chilling is effective during that time. The process is called "vernalization" or "thermoperiodicity."

DIRECT SEEDING OF TOMATOES: While the seeds of most tomato varieties must be started indoors weeks ahead of frost-free date in the garden, there are new varieties which can be planted right out in the garden and still produce bountiful crops within your growing season. This is called direct seeding, and many commercial growers are doing it. Plant after May 10 in the north, after March 20 in the south, and after April in the middle states. Be sure to start with the earliest variety possible.

Turnips
(B R A S S I C A R A P A)

This hairy-leaved biennial has been gaining in favor with home gardeners who like the leaves for greens and the boiled roots. More popular in Europe than in America.

HISTORICAL FACTS: Turnips have been in cultivation since before the Christian era and are probably native to central Asia. They spread across Asia to the Pacific.

STARTING SEED: Turnips have the same cultural tips as rutabagas. You can plant seed in late July for a fall crop. They do best on rather light soil of high fertility. Sown in July or August, turnips will be much better quality than those sown early. We sow our turnips on land from which an early crop such as peas or spinach has been harvested earlier in the season. Sow seeds in rows 12 to 15 inches apart, cover lightly, and thin to stand 3 to 4 inches in the row. Or you can just broadcast (scatter) seed, sowing thinly. Harvest in late summer, when roots are about 2 or 3 inches in diameter. Plants are hardy and may be left in ground until severe freezing weather comes in fall.

Watermelons
(CITRULLUS VULGARIS)

"Ice box" watermelons were bred especially for people who have no room for giant melons and have small growing spaces. They can be grown on fences, in pots, or tubs if given a trellis for support. For the yellow flesh variety try Golden Honey or Yellow Baby or one of the newer ones. You can also grow the red-flesh types such as Hampshire Midget or Sugar Baby. Another easy and small melon is the Takii Gem (pronounced "Tocky"). Bush-type melons are available where a normal vine melon takes several feet to run. Bush types can be grown in one-quarter the space.

HISTORICAL FACTS: The watermelon has been in cultivation for over 4,000 years. It is a native of Central Africa. Growing wild and cultivated in Africa, it has been an important water source in times of drought.

STARTING SEED: Start plants indoors in peat pots or Jiffy pellets, three weeks ahead of the time that is safe to set outdoors. Watermelons like it hot and they like plenty of water. Knowing when to pick a watermelon is a trick. Here are some indicators of ripeness: brown tendrils on the stem near the fruit; yellowish color where the melon touches the ground; rough and slightly ridged feel as you rub your hand over the melon. Most melons give a metallic ringing sound when they are green, and a muffled or dead sound as they get mature.

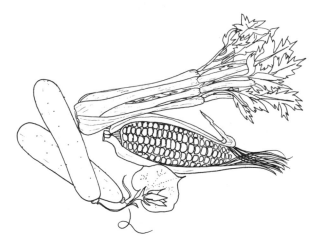

ANNUALS

ANNUALS ARE THE CHEAPEST YET SHOWIEST OF ALL garden flowers. A dollar's worth of seed produces hundreds of dollars' worth of enjoyment with a minimum of effort. The selection of annuals today is the best ever. Seedsmen have spent millions of dollars producing new varieties. You can thank the Bedding Plant Growers of America (now called Professional Plant Growers) for their efforts to give you the best selections possible.

Annuals, sold as bedding plants, complete their growth in one year, and thus are started from seed every year. Before you order seed, consider what effect you want and if your plants will be grown in sun or shade. Remember: An elaborate color scheme is not necessary. Select two or three good combinations and place them where they'll show off best. In a hanging basket or pot you can have a combination of colors and get a real show.

In planning your annual bed, don't make the mistake of making it too wide. Against a fence, a 4- or 5-foot width is handy, and in the open, 6 or 7 feet is sufficient. Over greater distances, it's difficult to pick the flowers or work the beds. Also, order taller plants for use behind the shorter ones. Most annuals need at least 6 hours of sunshine for best growth. Petunias, salvia, asters, and even gernaiums will take some afternoon shade. Begonias, coleus, and impatiens do best in dappled shade.

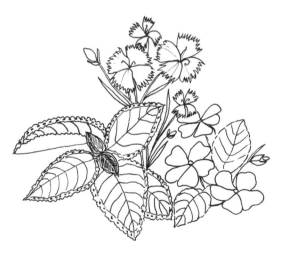

Time to Start Annuals

The cheapest way to get a lot of plants is to grow them yourself from seed. Use a hotbed or cold frame or greenhouse to start your own and discover the joy of seeing plants come from seed. There are some you can sow directly in the ground outdoors, but in the north most annuals get a head start and do best if started indoors in the spring. Some annuals are fall sown, although this practice is not too popular. Those started indoors vary in their rate of germination and development.

When you order seed, note how many seeds are in a packet. You could be getting too many or not enough. Whatever you do get will be a bargain because seed is relatively inexpensive. For example, if you bought four packets of salvia seed, you'd have about 400 seeds for what you would spend for a dozen or fifteen started plants from a garden store. If all 400 seeds germinated, you'd get about 33 dozen plants—enough for the whole neighborhood.

Outdoor Sowing

When sowing in the garden where the plants are to remain, it is a good plan to drop 3 or 4 seeds together in groups or hills 6 to 10 inches apart. When the seedlings come through, thin them to the one or two best plants in each group. This prevents overcrowding and permits proper cultivation. Always keep in mind the ultimate size of the well-grown plant and allow plenty of room.

The proper time for outdoor sowing of most annuals is about the time the trees start to leaf out. A few flowers such as zinnias, marigolds, nasturtiums, and portulaca require warm soil for germination and should be sown about a week or two later. Sweet peas and larkspur should be sown earlier, or just as soon as the ground can be worked.

In general, quick-germinating annuals such as zinnias, marigolds, candytuft, etc., will give good results if the seed is sown directly in the ground outdoors. Slow-growing kinds such as hybrid petunia, snapdragons, impatiens, etc., are best handled by starting the seed indoors.

Fall Sowing of Flower Seed

Sowing annual flower seed in the fall is, at best, undependable in the northern latitude, but if you succeed, the exceedingly hardy plants you get in the spring will be well worth the effort. Even a small percentage of success is worth it.

The area where the seed is sown should be well protected from winds and so situated that it will catch all the snow possible. The soil should be exceptionally well drained and of a character and location that warms quickly in the spring. A warm, well-drained, sandy soil with a slight slope that is protected by shrubs or buildings on three sides except the south is ideal. Lacking such an area, we recommend that you build a frame 1 foot high around the seed bed and cover it in the winter with boards and brush.

When to sow is always problematic. Annual larkspur may be planted as early as September 10. Such a sowing will produce small plants that will, under favorable conditions, withstand the winter. All other fall-sown annuals, however, should not be sown until just before the ground freezes so that the seed will lie dormant over the winter and commence to sprout with the first warm rains of spring.

Do not bury the seed: Merely stir it into the surface of well-prepared soil and cover the seedbed with light brush, such as shrub trimmings. Calendulas, cosmos, pansies, dianthus, snapdragon, and alyssum are some annuals that can be sown in fall. Avoid the most common reasons for failure.

1. Do not cover the seed too deeply.
2. Do not plant in heavy soil that will form a crust over the seed.
3. Do not allow the soil to dry out, but do not overwater.
4. Do not plant tender varieties in soil that is too cold.
5. Do not plant too thickly.

Here are some annuals we consider best for the home garden. These will give you plenty of color and show with the least amount of effort.

Ageratum
(AGERATUM)

One of the few good blue flowers, ageratum is ideal for

borders, edges of rock gardens, and porch boxes. It grows 8 to 12 inches tall in white, off-pink, and blue. The tall 24-inch blue variety is good for borders and cutting.

GREEN THUMB CARE: Plant 6 to 8 inches apart in full sun or semishade. Cut off faded flowers to keep plants looking handsome. In dry soils, plants will wilt. When flowers turn brown, snip them off.

STARTING SEED: Start indoors 3 to 4 months before planting outdoors.

Aster, China
(CALLISTEPHUS CHINENSIS)

Here's a fine late summer and early fall cut flower in all shades of lavender, salmon, crimson, light pink, deep rose, white, and cream. Available varieties range from 10 inches to 3 feet in height. Asters are ideal for bouquets and bedding plants.

GREEN THUMB CARE: Asters like full sun, but do well in partial shade where insect activity is reduced. They need well-drained, fairly rich soil.

STARTING SEED: Sow indoors 6 weeks before outdoor planting. After seedlings are about 2 inches high, transplant to a seed flat or, after danger of frost, to the garden.

Begonia
(BEGONIA)

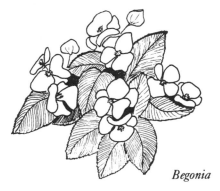

Begonia

Along with impatiens, hybrid wax begonias have climbed to the top in popularity as a bedding plant. They do not have the color range of petunias, but they are more versatile because they can be grown in sun or semishade. They provide a neat, bright display all summer long without the gardener pinching them or worrying about seed pods. The F1 hybrids start flowering when plants are very small and continue throughout the summer, whether it's hot or cool, wet or dry. Begonias are self-cleaning, meaning they drop their old flowers as new ones appear.

GREEN THUMB CARE: Begonias like a well-drained soil with humus and good air circulation to prevent mildew in late summer.

STARTING SEED: Sow in one of the soilless mixes. Seeds are like dust so it helps to mix them with a small quantity of white sand in a saltshaker. Then shake this mix on the soil to get even distribution. Do not cover with soil; you might want to apply a very light dusting of vermiculite (use the horticultural grade, not the kind found in lumber yards). Mist the seed with warm water and place in a temperature of 72 degrees F. Sow 18 weeks before outdoor planting.

Begonia, Nonstop Hybrid

A cross between a small single-bloom begonia and tuberous begonias, these are one of the most sensational innovations in flower breeding. Seeds will produce a blooming plant in four to five months. They come in a spectacular range of colors and bloom continuously all summer outdoors and can be grown indoors if given good light. They form tubers which can be saved. Seeds germinate at 65 degrees F., but must be under fluorescent lights for good germination. As with regular begonia seeds, they must be sprinkled on top of Peat-Lite–type mix and kept moist.

Calendula
(POT OR SCOTCH MARIGOLD)

This is one of the most durable annuals for the home garden. It will often self-sow and come up the following spring. Try some of the newer varieties which produce uniformly large, well-formed flowers with long, straight stems. Calendulas are ideal for cut flowers.

GREEN THUMB CARE: They will take hot weather if seed heads are cut off; this allows flowers to continue after frost.

STARTING SEED: Start seed indoors, then transplant to pots and set outdoors after frost. Make a second sowing outdoors in early July and you will have flowers in late summer and fall.

Cleome
(SPIDER FLOWER)

Cleome is a tall, bold annual 4 to 5 feet in height which blooms from June to frost. The Rose Queen develops huge heads of delightful true pink. Equally showy is Helen Campbell, a pure white. A purple variety is available, too. The four-petaled flowers have an airy appearance because of their unusual long-stemmed stamens and pistils (male and female floral parts). It's ideal as a background plant.

GREEN THUMB CARE: Cleome grows in poor soils, but flowers are fuller if plants are watered twice a week or so.

STARTING SEED: Seed may be started indoors at 70 degrees F. 4 weeks before setting outdoors. Some gardeners sow outdoors when the weather permits. Cleome self-sows readily.

Cockscomb
(CELOSIA)

A good flower for the gardener who wants something different. Plant breeders have done a fine job developing new varieties of both the crested types (like a rooster's comb) and the plumed type (*plumosa*), which are feathery spikes. Both types come in colors besides fiery red, which is the most popular variety and makes a dazzling show when used alone or combined with white flowers. Gardeners have a choice of foliage color: glossy green or a bronze-red.

GREEN THUMB CARE: Cockscomb needs plenty of space (12 to 18 inches) since crowding decreases the size of the heads. It will bloom prematurely with small heads if the growth of young plants is checked. Do not start plants too early indoors, as growth will be checked before transplanting. Do not sow outdoors until soil has warmed up thoroughly.

STARTING SEED: Sow seed in small flats and transplant seedlings when they are 1½ inches tall. It germinates at 70 degrees F.

Coleus

Coleus is an easy-to-grow houseplant and bedding plant ideal for porch pots, boxes, etc. It's one of the showiest things to grow in outdoor shade. New varieties are out of this world. Some leaves are highly colored—olive, bronze, burgundy, golden, chartreuse flecked with green, rose, red, pastel shades, and almost any color mixture you want.

GREEN THUMB CARE: Although coleus will tolerate sun, it prefers semishade. Companion plants to grow with coleus in shade include begonias (both annual and tuberous), impatiens, and browallia. Coleus likes a loose, well-drained soil. If flower spikes appear, pinch them off as soon as they begin. This gives you a stockier plant. Too much direct sun will cause leaves to blanch. Dropping of leaves can be due to dry soil and dry air. Brown edges and tips are caused by hot sun or hot air.

STARTING SEED: Start seed in Peat-Lite–type soil or soilless soil mix. Sow thinly, do not cover (or just dust), and press lightly into the soil. It likes light for germination and a temperature of 72 degrees F. or more and never less than 65 degrees F. Keep soil uniformly moistened. When seedlings show up, don't be disappointed—they all are green at first, but start showing color when the third set of true leaves appear.

Cosmos

Cosmos is an attractive, airy background plant. If you are a new home owner and want a quick-growing item while your small woody ornamentals are getting established, consider the cosmos. It grows 4 feet tall with large daisylike flowers in clear white, pink, rose, orchid, and crimson. Orange and yellow varieties are smaller bloomed and some are shorter.

GREEN THUMB CARE: After plants are 2 feet tall, pinch back to induce side branches to form. Pinching delays blooming, so don't pinch too late or you won't get blooms. They like a well-drained soil and full sun. Avoid heavy feeding as they don't need too rich a soil. Some may need staking to prevent wind damage.

STARTING SEED: Start seed outdoors in May after frost. Thin plants to 18 inches apart for nice husky plants. You can also start seed indoors for early blooming. Allow only 2 weeks before setting out or they will get too tall.

Dahlia

Today tall varieties and dwarf annual dahlias come in rich and varied colors. Seed-grown dahlias are earlier to bloom and will form tubers, which are handled like those of the giant or larger dahlias. Flowers are double, semidouble, and single, and are ideal for short cut flowers all summer long and for long-flowering bedding plants.

GREEN THUMB CARE: Seed dahlias need regular watering during the summer months. Keep spent blooms pinched off for continuous bloom. If ends of stems are dipped in hot water for about a minute after cutting, the cut flowers will last for days.

STARTING SEED: Seed sown directly outdoors after danger of frost will bloom in late summer. For earlier bloom, start seed indoors or in a cold frame about

4 weeks earlier than outdoor planting time. As far as we know, all seed packages have mixed colors.

Gerbera
(TRANSVAAL DAISY)

If you live in a warm climate, gerbera (also spelled geberia) is a perennial. In cold regions, it's grown as an annual. It's popular with florists as a cut flower because of its strong stems and graceful, long-lasting single and double blooms. Gerberas are ideal grown in a greenhouse, outdoors in a summer border, or in a pot. From varieties listed as double flowering, one can usually expect 75 percent doubles.

STARTING SEED: Start seeds indoors in February for summer bloom. Sow seed in loose mixture at 72 degrees F. and transplant each one to a 3-inch pot and set outdoors in warm weather.

Impatiens
(DAY PLANT OR SULTANA)

No annual has gained so fast in popularity as this shady lady. If you want a riot of color for shady (or sunny) areas, nothing is better. Impatiens (im-PAY-shunz) are extremely tolerant of air pollution. Solid colors, variegated, and bicolor blooms produce a spectacular show. Both dwarf and taller hybrids come in shades of crimson, fuchsia, orange, orchid, pink, rose, salmon, scarlet,

Impatiens

and white. Double-flowered varieties are also available. All types are suitable for hanging baskets, window boxes, porch pots, and even as houseplants. Like begonias they are self-cleaning, so there are no faded blooms to remove.

GREEN THUMB CARE: All varieties will tolerate a rather poor soil, but they do better in a loose, well-balanced soil. Some varieties can be grown in full sun with abundant watering, but all plants prefer some shade at least part of the day. They will not tolerate poor drainage. Dwarfs grow to a height of 8 to 10 inches and are base-branching, meaning you don't have to pinch them for bushiness. The taller types grow from 12 to 20 inches high and should be pinched for bushy plants—just snip out the tip and root it in water for another plant.

STARTING SEED: Sow seeds 8 to 10 weeks before you want to plant outdoors in a loose mix such as half perlite, vermiculite, or sharp sand and peat moss or one of the prepared sterile mixes. Do not cover with soil, as they need light to germinate. For transplanting, we use a mixture of two parts perlite, vermiculite, or sand; 1 part organic matter (peat moss or compost); and 1 part loam. Remember: A loose soil mix dries out fast and may need frequent watering. For winter bloom indoors, take cuttings from outdoor blooming plants in early fall and root them in water.

Impatiens, New Guinea

These hybrids are new to many gardeners but are gaining in popularity all over. They were developed in the 1970s by the USDA and Longwood Gardens researchers, who bred and cross-bred several species of wild impatiens collected from the jungles and mountains of Papua, New Guinea. Several of the hybrids have colorfully variegated or glossy deep green or bronze foliage, whereas common impatiens have plain light green leaves. The New Guinea impatiens are propagated from cuttings or seeds. Both are somewhat expensive—individual plants may run between $1.25 and $2.75—but because of their unique beauty, they are well worth it. These plants will be cheaper as more and more seed companies develop and perfect seed. The seed does not stay viable for very long. In a seed breeding program, an effort is being made to get seed to come true and last longer. Ball Seed Company has a New Guinea impatiens seed series called Spectrum. Park Seed Company and others have New Guinea hybrid seed. The American gardener is clamoring for hybrids from seed and soon they will be plentiful and cheaper. Seed-starting directions are the same as for regular impatiens.

Kale and Cabbage, Flowering

Plant breeders have done wonders with these relatively new ornamentals, which begin to color up when other summer annuals wane. Called "ornamental" kale and cabbage, these striking plants are used for accent or pattern plantings and also for potted plants. They are handsome in combination with chrysanthemums. They relish cool temperatures and will withstand 20 degrees F. with improved color and vigor. Bright pink, red, and white varieties of "flowering" (they are not actual flowers) kale are available in frilled and deeply serrated, feathery varieties (such as Frizzy and Peacock). Ornamental cabbage is more like a mammoth old-fashioned rose, and available colors are just as striking as those of kale. All varieties are bordered by handsome green leaves.

GREEN THUMB CARE: Plants can be grown in containers or beds. They need ample moisture and sunshine to obtain full color. Overfeeding may cause dull coloration.

STARTING SEED: Seeds prefer light for good germination and a temperature of 70 degrees F. Start them

5 to 7 weeks before you want to transplant outdoors. For movable pots, transplant some into 2½-inch pots to be moved to 6- to 8-inch azalea pots later on. These are handy for moving around your property or moving indoors for centerpieces for special occasions.

Larkspur
(ANNUAL DELPHINIUM)

Ideal for cut flowers, larkspur has lovely, branchy, 3-foot stalks of single or double florets, with white, pink, and shades of lavender. The regal strain produces large, compact blooms on long stems. "Hardy larkspur" is a perennial delphinium. New varieties do not lose petals as easily as the older types.

STARTING SEED: Sow in the early spring outdoors or indoors for late summer bloom or in the fall for next June's bloom. It needs a cool temperature (60 degrees F.) for germination.

Marigold
(TAGETES)

Marigold

Gardeners have a bewildering number of marigolds to choose from: tall mum types, short mum types, carnation-flowered and ball-flowered; large flowered dwarf, dwarf single, and dwarf double-flowering types; African (*erecta*) and French (*patula*). Marigolds are ideal for urns, porch boxes, background plantings, and edgings along drives and walks. Few annuals are more dependable. They come in all shades of yellow, orange, gold, bronze, and even white. Bicolors are prevalent among new varieties.

GREEN THUMB CARE: Marigolds thrive in almost any kind of soil. They need sun and bloom continuously in summer heat—especially the dwarf and semidwarf types. Foliage is strong smelling, but there are odorless varieties. Pick off seed heads for continuous bloom. Some large-flowering marigolds bloom late, so be sure to buy early flowering types if you get early frosts.

Tall varieties are affected by day length and some won't blossom until days are shorter in the fall. Some hybrids will flower earlier, so order these if you want earlier blooms. If dwarf edging marigolds fail to bloom, check buds for thrips and tarnished plant bugs. Spray with Malathion or Sevin in the bud stage. Spider mites can cause mottled and brown foliage. Look for cobwebs on tips. Spray with buttermilk spray or syringe with water daily.

STARTING SEED: Start seed indoors about 4 weeks before you want to plant outdoors. Separate the seedlings when 1½ to 2 inches high and plant them in boxes or flats of loose soil or transplant them directly to soil outdoors.

If you're a marigold lover, you might want to join the Marigold Society of America. They publish the *Amerigold Newsletter,* which is full of information about this popular bedding plant. The address is:

Miss Jeannette Lowe
394 West Court St.
Doylestown, PA 18933

Morning Glory
(IPOMOEA)

Although there are red, white, and blue varieties, Heavenly Blue is still the favorite of this popular annual vine that thrives in poor soil and grows almost anywhere, as long as it has sun. In dull weather the flowers stay open most of the day, but on sunny days they close up about noon. Very hot weather wilts the leaves, but they snap back. Morning glory makes a good screening vine.

Moonflowers are a form of morning glory with larger vines, larger leaves, and huge, fragrant white flowers.

GREEN THUMB CARE: They like a soil that is

not too fertile and they need a fence or trellis to climb on. Morning glories bloom more freely if the tips are nipped before the first buds form; this forces the growth of side shoots, which bloom profusely.

STARTING SEED: Morning glories have a hard seed coat. To aid germination, soak seed overnight in warm water (or file a notch in the seed). Sow outdoors after danger of frost, in the place where they are to remain, or sow them in individual peat pots or Jiffy-7 pellets indoors, so roots will not be disturbed when planting outdoors. Start 2 or 3 weeks before the outdoor planting date. Seed germinates irregularly, so don't give up easily. Plant 3 or 4 seeds in each pot. If all germinate, let 2 remain in each pot.

Nasturtium
(TROPAEOLUM)

This old-fashioned plant remains popular. In fact, 1989 was called the Year of the Nasturtium. Some folks like the leaves in sandwiches and salads and the seeds pickled.

GREEN THUMB CARE: Nasturtiums tolerate semishade and are ideal for poor soil and hot weather. The tall type is ideal for trellises, window boxes, wall covering, and hanging baskets. Flowers are orange, yellow, red, and variegated. They will climb to considerable height during the summer if given support. Don't sow in too rich a soil or you will get mostly leaves and few or no flowers.

There are dwarf semidouble varieties with short runners; the globe type, which makes a compact plant; and varieties with variegated leaves. Dwarf Jewel is a dandy, with fragrant flowers well above foliage. There are also green and white variegated nasturtiums. If you've got an old stump that needs hiding, plant a few nasturtium seeds in soil on it and let the plants cover the stump.

STARTING SEED: Start seed indoors 3 weeks ahead of outdoor planting time, in Jiffy-7 pots, or sow outdoors in late spring.

Petunia

Until recently the petunia was the most popular annual in America. Now it has been dethroned by impatiens. It's still a great bedding plant and the new varieties are better than ever.

Here are some reasons petunias have lost out in popularity. Petunias need more care than some other annuals; they often get straggly by midsummer, and they do not stand up as well in hot or rainy weather. However, their many colors, types of growth, and the vigor of the many hybrids—especially the double multiflora types—still make them favorites. Whether you want to use them in pots, beds, hanging baskets, or window boxes, there is a petunia that has been developed especially for the purpose.

Petunia classification is so confusing that even expert gardeners have a hard time deciding which kind to select.

. . . Grandiflora (giant flower): large-flowered, including varieties with fringed, waved, and plain edges. This class includes both F1 hybrids and open-pollinated varieties.

. . . Multiflora (many flowered): Smaller-flowered or bedding F1 hybrids that bloom in great profusion.

. . . Dwarf bedding or nana compacta: Open-pollinated, small-flowered types. Usually flowers less freely and is not as uniform as F1 hybrids.

. . . Balcony type: Denotes a use rather than a single class; all varieties growing 14 inches or more can be used.

. . . Double-flowered: These have more than one row of petals. They include both the large double varieties (grandifloras) with flowers up to 5 inches across and the smaller kinds, sometimes called carnation-flowered or multifloras with 2- to 3-inch flowers.

GREEN THUMB CARE: Petunias like full sun and ample water in the summer. Don't just remove faded blooms; pinch off the seed pods as well to maintain plant vigor. If faded blossoms and pods are picked off, the plants will keep right on blooming.

STARTING SEED: Start indoors in early spring or late winter using a soilless mix. Sow thinly and do not cover, press the seed in lightly and water by submerging the seed flat in a shallow pan. Single types need 70 degrees F. for germination. Since double petunia seedlings develop a little more slowly than singles, their seed should be sown indoors about 2½ to 3 months before outdoor planting time. They need 75 degrees F. to germinate well. All petunias need light for germination.

Portulaca
(MOSS ROSE)

This is a gay and accommodating flower that grows in the poorest and driest ground as long as it gets plenty of sun. It seeds itself and is unrivaled for brilliance among plants of low growth. The flowers open only in full sun, closing at night and on cloudy days. The succulent, needly foliage has a creeping habit. It is ideal for lining sidewalks and driveways, and for planting around garages, on sunny banks, and even between stepping stones. Some gardeners broadcast the seed over rock gardens to fill them with color. It can also cover bare spots and stumps. Portulaca grows 3 to 6 inches tall and bears single and double flowers in red, pink, rose, yellow, white, and shades in between.

GREEN THUMB CARE: Keep weeds out. Avoid heavy watering.

STARTING SEED: Sow seed outdoors after soil is warm. Scatter seed on the surface and thin plants later to 6 inches apart. It blooms in 6 weeks and continues until frost. Portulaca self-sows, but the doubles revert to singles even though colors remain vivid. It can also be started indoors 8 weeks before transplanting out doors. A temperature of 70 degrees F. is needed for good germination.

Salvia
(SCARLET SAGE)

Few plants are more striking in a mass than salvia. You will also like the brilliant red flowers planted among evergreens or in borders.

There's a world of difference in the habit of growth and blossoming dates of the several types available. The early dwarf (12 inches tall) blooms from mid-July until frost. The intermediate type grows about 16 inches high, and blooms from early August until frost. Late salvia blooms from mid-August until frost and grows 24 to 30 inches tall. Blue *Salvia farinacea* has long, graceful spikes with long stems in an attractive shade of light blue; it is ideal for cutting. White is available, also. These plants require the same care as scarlet salvia and will continue to flower right up until late fall.

GREEN THUMB CARE: Keep watered in the summer and grow in full sun. Besides red, *Salvia splendens* now comes in violet, white, and salmon.

STARTING SEED: Start indoors in early spring. Sow seed 10 to 12 weeks before outdoor planting. Light is needed for good germination. Do not plant outdoors until all danger of frost is over.

Snapdragon
(A N T I R R H I N U M)

Snapdragon

These are available in a variety of excellent colors. There are tall and dwarf varieties, but the medium-height varieties are best for general purposes. The more you cut the spikes, the more the plants produce.

The hybrids are the earliest to bloom, branch more freely, and have an upright habit of growth, enabling them to withstand moderate winds without support. The new tetraploids ("tetras") have larger flowers and taller, stronger stems than regular varieties. They are not rust resistant, however. Butterfly (open-faced) types have become popular. They are available in tall and dwarf sizes as well as single and double blooms. For an edging, you might want to try the floral carpet snaps.

GREEN THUMB CARE: Plants will be leggy unless you pinch them back when 2 inches high. For husky seedlings, grow in a cool place. They will withstand frost after hardening. Grow in sun in well-drained soil. Dwarf plants produce up to 25 little 3-inch spikes all in bloom at once. Shear each one off after blooming to extend the display.

STARTING SEED: Sow indoors in March for outdoor planting. The seed is fine and has little pushing-up power. Sow in loose soil and cover lightly (just sift fine peat moss over the seed). Light needs to penetrate the covering for good germination.

Stock
(MATTHIOLA)

Everyone likes the spicy fragrance of stocks, but not everyone can get this plant to bloom outdoors. Stocks like cool weather and must be started indoors or they may not bloom when warm weather rolls around. The Trysomic Seven Week stocks have been bred for earliness and ability to stand up under summer heat. They grow 20 to 30 inches high, producing fragrant stems which branch out into bushy plants. The so-called double Ten Week stocks are favorites for outdoor growing and bloom 10 weeks after sowing. The long-lasting flowers are ideal for vase arrangements and come in a variety of colors: white, lavender, purple, light pink, rose, red, and cream. All have fragrant blooms. A midget series is now available, which can be grown in pots or used for bedding.

GREEN THUMB CARE: No pinching is necessary. Remove spent blossoms when cutting for bouquets. (Pound the stem ends of cut flowers with a hammer or knife handle to help them take up water better.)

STARTING SEED: Seed can be sown indoors or outdoors. Sow indoors 9 to 10 weeks before you intend to set transplants in the garden. The best germinating temperature is 65 to 75 degrees F.

Sweet Alyssum
(LOBULARIA MARITIMA)

A fast-growing, dainty little plant recommended for use in borders, edgings, baskets, pots, and rock gardens. They grow to a height of 3 to 6 inches. White alyssum is a prolific plant that sows seeds which live over the winter. Pink and purple varieties do not often self-sow. There are two types: dwarf upright, such as Little Gem, Violet Queen, and Rosie O'Day, and the procumbent type such as Carpet-of-Snow and Royal Carpet. There's also a new variety, a cross between white and purple, which shows these colors on the same plant.

STARTING SEED: Seed is small and should be covered lightly, if at all. Some gardeners cover the row with a strip of newspaper after sowing. The newspaper keeps the soil moist and insures a good stand. You can also start seed indoors 8 weeks before outdoor planting time.

If sown outdoors after warm weather arrives, sweet alyssum will bloom in 6 weeks.

Sweet Pea
(L A T H Y R U S   O D O R A T U S)

This is one of the very few fragrant annuals. Cuthbertson and Royal Family varieties (spring-flowering strains) are quite heat resistant. Floribundas and multifloras are free flowering and long stemmed. Spencer types are good for the home garden, especially where summers are not too hot. Bush sweet peas are useful in borders, window boxes, and baskets. Little Sweetheart is one of the best; plants grow only 8 inches tall, produce large, fragrant flowers, and are very heat resistant. Mammoth has become a favorite; plants grow 2½ feet tall and produce large, straight stems of fragrant blooms in a full range of colors—salmon, scarlet, rose, white, cerise, blue, and crimson. They are ideal for cut flower arrangements. Snoopea and Super Snoop are sturdy dwarfs. Bijou is a bush type that grows 12 to 18 inches tall with early, long-lasting flowers in a complete color range.

GREEN THUMB CARE: Sweet peas need sunlight and plenty of water. Being a legume, they need lime applied at rate of half a pound to a 15-foot row. Also add 1 pound of complete plant food to a 15-foot row. Pick flowers daily or vines will wither. If many seed pods form, the vine will die. Cut flowers in the morning before sun hits them. If blooms wilt after picking, hold stems under warm water and cut off an inch or two; they'll recover in 30 minutes. With trailing types, support vines when plants are 4 inches high, because if they topple over they seldom do as well again. Chicken wire or twiggy branches stuck in both sides of the row give good support.

STARTING SEED: Sow seed outdoors in fall or early spring. Dig soil deep and work in generous amounts of humus, but not manure (to avoid Botrytis blight). Sow seeds 2 inches apart in a furrow 2 or 3 inches deep, and cover lightly with loose soil. After plants are 4 or 5 inches high, give them a side dressing of 5-10-5 fertilizer. A feeding of liquid plant food when they are in bud brings about a longer blooming season. White seeds seem to rot more readily than the tinted ones, and very dark seeds usually have a harder coat and take longer to germinate. Nick each seed with a file before sowing. If your seed rots in the ground, try presprouting it: place the seed in a moist medium, such as wet cotton or shallow pans of water for 3 to 5 days at 65 to 70 degrees F.

An alternative is to sow in Jiffy-7 pellets or pots with peat mix. Be sure to cover seeds, as they like darkness for germination. Keep them moist. They germinate in a temperature of 55 degrees F. since they are a cool-weather crop. It may take 10 to 15 days to see the sprouts. They can be planted in the garden anytime but it is best not to let seedlings get too tall.

Sunflower
(HELIANTHUS ANNUUS)

Sunflowers are some flowers! This species was a treasured plant of the American Indians. While not a vegetable, it's surprising to see how many gardeners raise this item for ornamental use and food as well. A row of sunflowers makes a fine "living" fence on which birds may feed.

STARTING SEED: Sow seed outdoors in the spring after the soil warms and by summer you can have plants 15 feet tall. They like heat and plenty of moisture. Flower size can vary from 4 inches to 12 inches across. Height ranges from 2 to 10 feet or more. Besides the typical gold color, flowers can be had in primrose, red, and bronze. The short, multiflowered types make good background flowers for beds.

Zinnia

Zinnia

The zinnia is perhaps the best all-purpose annual. In its native country, Mexico, it was called "eyesore" plant because the original flowers were a dirty orange or washed-out magenta. The plant has been dramatized and hybridized so that we now have a bewildering color range. There is a large range of heights and bloom size. Zinnias get a disease known as alternaria blight, manifested by brown spots that cause leaves to parch and dry up completely. No chemical controls this, but some varieties are more resistant than others; these include Liliputs (Pompons), cut-and-come-again types, and State Fair.

GREEN THUMB CARE: The crown flower (the first to appear) can be cut early, forcing the blooms on the side branches to grow larger. Give them full sun. If the soil becomes infected with the alternaria blight, the fungus will survive the winter and infect plants again the following season, even if you start with perfectly healthy plants. Do not grow zinnias in the same spot year after year.

STARTING SEED: Zinnia seeds germinate in 4 or 5 days indoors at 70 degrees F., giving you flowers 40 days after sowing. You can also start them outdoors directly in the garden. Do not sow seed too thickly; thin the seedlings or plants will be skinny.

Other Bonus Annuals

Pansy   Lobelia

The preceding list of annuals was shortened reluctantly. There are dozens of other blue-ribbon annuals we'd like to see you grow in your garden. These include amaranth (Joseph's coat); anchusa (summer forget-me-not); baby's breath (*Gypsophila*); bachelor's button or cornflower (*Centaurea cyanus*); balsam; bells of Ireland (*Molucella laevis*); California poppy (*Eschscholtzia californica*); castor bean (*Ricinus*); chrysanthemum (annual); clarkia; datura (angel's trumpet); dianthus (annual pink) four o'clock (*Mirabilis*); gaillardia (blanket flower); globe amaranth (*Gomphrena globosa*); helichrysum (straw flower); hibiscus (annual mallow); kochia (summer cypress); *Lavatera* (Loveliness); lobelia; mi-

HELPFUL INFORMATION FOR STARTING ANNUALS

Plant	Best Germinating Temperature (in °F.)	Light or Darkness Needed	Number of Days for Germination	Time to Start Indoors for Outdoor Planting (Weeks)
Ageratum (reg. varieties)	70	Light	5	12 to 16
Alyssum	70	Either	5	12 to 16
Aster (annual)	70	Either	15	4 to 6
Begonia (fibrous-rooted)	70	Light	15	18 to 22
Browallia	70	Light	15	12 to 16
Calendula (pot marigold)	70	Dark	10	4 to 6
Carnation (annual)	70	Either	20	12 to 16
Celosia (cockscomb)	70	Either	10	6 to 8
Centaurea (cornflower)	65	Dark	10	8 to 10
Coleus	70	Light	10	8 to 10
Cosmos	70	Either	5	6 to 8
Dahlia (from seed)	70	Either	5	10 to 12
Dianthus (annual pinks)	70	Either	5	12 to 16
Dusty miller (Cineraria)	70	Light	10	12 to 14
Gaillardia (annual)	70	Either	20	12 to 16
Geranium (seed)	75	Either	5 to 10	18 to 20

Plant				
Heliotrope	70	Either	25	10 to 12
Hollyhock (annual)	60	Either	10	12 to 16
Impatiens (sultana or day plant)	70	Light	15	9 to 12
Lobelia	70	Either	20	15 to 22
Marigold (dwarf types)	70	Either	5	6 to 10
Marigold (tall types)	70	Either	5	6 to 10
Nicotiana (fl. tobacco)	70	Light	20	4 to 6
Nierembergia (dwarf cup flower)	70	Either	15	10 to 12
Pansy	65	Dark	10	22 to 26
Petunia	70	Light	10	10 to 15
Phlox drummondii (annual)	65	Dark	10	8 to 12
Portulaca (moss rose)	70	Dark	15	6 to 8
Rudbeckia (coneflower)	70	Either	10	10 to 12
Salvia splendens	70	Light	15	8 to 14
Silver feather	75	Either	14 to 21	18 to 22
Snapdragon	70	Light	10	12 to 14
Sweet pea	55	Dark	15	8 to 10
Verbena	65	Dark	20	8 to 10
Vinca rosea (periwinkle)	70	Dark	15	10 to 2
Zinnia	70	Either	5	4 to 6

CHART 3.1

GUIDELINES FOR ANNUALS

The following chart showing seeding and transplanting times may be used as a rough guide for those who want to start their own seeds in the spring. It is a rough guide because conditions differ from house to house and differ again from greenhouse to greenhouse. Every grower eventually develops his or her own guide and it is suggested that a record be maintained yearly.

Name	Seeding Time	Germination Time	Transplant Time	Remarks
Ageratum	Apr. 1	4–5 days	May 1	After transplanting keep cool at about 60 degrees.
Alyssum	Mar. 1	3–4 days	Apr. 1	Transplant in clumps.
Aster	Apr. 15	7 days	May 10	Do not transplant too deep.
Balsam	Apr. 15	5 days	Apr. 25	Keep on the dry side.
Carnation	Mar. 15	7 days	Apr. 15	Keep cool. Plant very shallow.
Cleome	Apr. 15	10–12 days	May 10	Likes warm days, cool nights.
Coleus	Mar. 15	7 days	Apr. 15	Do not plant too deep. Likes shade.
Dahlia	Apr. 15	3–4 days	May 15	
Dianthus	Mar. 15	8–10 days	Apr. 15	Dampens off easily.
Geranium (soak seed)	Jan. 15	8 days	Feb. 15	Transplant when small; do not check growth.
Impatiens	Mar. 7	8 days	Apr. 1	Needs light to germinate.
Lobelia	Mar. 1	3 days	Apr. 1	Sow thin; transplant in clumps.
Marigold (dwarf cupid)	Feb. 15	3 days	Mar. 15	Slow growing. Watch for damping off.

Marigold (dwarf petite)	Apr. 15	5 days	May 10	Easy to grow.
Marigold (tall varieties)	Apr. 25	3 days	May 5	Keep on dry side; needs full sun.
Nicotiana	Apr. 1	5 days	Apr. 20	Grows fast.
Pansy	Mar. 1	7 days	May 25	Keep cool.
Petunia (double)	Mar. 1	7 days	Apr. 1	Watch for damping-off.
Petunia (hybrid, multi, and grandiflora)	Mar. 15	5 days	Apr. 10	Sow thin; do not cover seeds.
Portulaca	Mar. 1	3 days	Apr. 1	
Ricinus	May 1–15	10 days		Sow directly to garden in peat pots.
Rudbeckia	Apr. 15	5 days	Mar. 15	Will reseed in garden.
Salvia	Mar. 15	5 days	Mar. 30	Transplant as soon as possible. Not easy to handle.
Snapdragon	Mar. 15	7 days	Apr. 15	Keep on cool side after transplanting.
Stock	Mar. 1	7 days	Apr. 1	Do not stall growth. Needs to be cooler after transplanting.
Verbena	Feb. 15	7 days	Mar. 20	Needs bottom heat. Requires good air circulation.
Zinnia	Apr. 10	2 days	Apr. 15	Transplant as soon as possible. Watch for damping-off.

CHART 3.2

gnonette (*Reseda*); nicotiana (flowering tobacco); nierembergia (cup flower); pansy; polygonum Orientale (kiss-me-over-the-garden-gate or prince's feather); poppy, Shirley (*Papaver rhoeas*); salpiglossis (painted tongue); sanvitalia (creeping zinnia); scabiosa (pincusion flower); schizanthus (poor man's orchid); statice (sea lavender, a half-hardy annual); sunflower, giant (*Helianthus annus*); tithonia (Mexican sunflower); verbena; and vinca (periwinkle).

4

PERENNIALS

IN RECENT YEARS THERE HAS BEEN A GREAT INTEREST in growing perennials in the backyard. One reason is that perennial seed is easier to get now, and there are more varieties than ever to choose from.

Perennials are the backbone of any permanent flower garden. Their roots live in the ground year after year, even though the tops die down each fall. These nearly ever-living plants are treasured not only for their long life but for their early response to warm spring days.

The cheapest way to get a perennial bed started is from seed. Many folks say they want a perennial garden because they want flowers that come up by themselves and don't require any care. There's no such thing. It takes time and effort to keep a perennial bed neat and attractive, but it's worth it, because with proper selection you can have beautiful flowers from early spring until frost. If you're going to sow perennial seed (and if your time is limited), select some of the best and easiest to grow. Choose carefully for size of plant, harmony of color, foliage habit, and season and length of blooms (see Chart 4.1). Beginners might start with eight "backbone" perennials for continuous flower display. These, in order of bloom, are: daffodils, tulips, iris, peonies, delphinium, perennial phlox, hardy lilies, and hardy mums. While most of these can be started from divisions, they can also be started from seed right in your own cold frame, kitchen window, or greenhouse. You may add others, but remember that a perennial border can be like a runaway horse if you grow too many types and let the beds get the best of you.

Before you spend a lot of money on seed, give some thought to the colors you want for effect. For example, orange and scarlet are stimulating colors that will attract attention. Green leaves are quiet and restful. Yellows are warm and invigorating. Blues are cool colors with greatest appeal in the warm, mid-summer months. There's no rule for arranging colors harmoniously, but one thing you can be sure of: green leaves are nature's peacemaker in the perennial garden and help make other colors blend together. It's better not to have more than two or three colors predominating at one time. Study seed catalogs for leaf texture. Large-leaved, coarse-branched plants don't look good mixed with small-leaved, fine-twigged plants. One of the real pleasures of a perennial garden comes from rearranging plants from time to time. Move them to get better harmony of color, form, and texture, as well as better seasonal effect.

Planning the Planting

Before you get your seed started, get your perennial bed in shape for spring planting. Dig up the soil thoroughly, mix in some fertilizer, compost, peat moss, humus, etc. The more organic matter you can incorporate into sandy or clay soil, the better it will be. Soils that bake hard in the summer or which are poorly drained are apt to give you trouble later. To get more mileage from your seed investment, make the perennial bed 4 or 5 feet wide and curve the border for effect. A bed 5 feet wide is as large as can be comfortably worked. Remember that perennials in masses are showier than those set out in a hit-or-miss fashion. And it doesn't do a bit of harm to repeat the same variety in a perennial bed. It will take years to get just the plants you want, so don't try to do it all in one year. *Be prepared to buy and sow more seed later.*

Chrysanthemum *Scabiosa (Pincushion flower)*

SIXTEEN POPULAR PERENNIALS TO GROW FROM SEED

Perennial	Sowing time outdoors	Germination time	Height	Flower Color	Bloom time
Achillea	Summer	10–14 days	18–24"	pink, yellow, peach, cream	Summer
Alyssum (basket of gold)	Spring	7 days	6"	golden	Spring
Anthemis	Summer	7 days	2'	golden	June–July
Aquilegia (columbine)	Spring, Summer	30days	18–24"	varied	Spring
Astilbe	Spring	14–21 days	2½–3'	pink, white	Summer
Chrysanthemum	Summer	7 days	6–4'	varied	Sept.–Oct.
Chrysanthemum maximum (shasta daisy)	Spring or Summer	10 days	2'	white	July
Coreopsis	Summer	21 days	1½'	yellow	Summer
Delphinium	Spring	18 days	1½–3'	blue, white, pink, lavender	June–July
Gaillardia (blanket flower)	Summer	21 days	2½'	bronze, gold, scarlet	June–Sept.
Liatris (gayfeather)	Spring	21 days	2–2½'	white, violet	July

Lobelia	Spring (after stratifying) or Fall	21 days	2'	red or blue	Aug. & Sept.
Rudbeckia (gloriosa daisy)	Summer	21 days	3'	bronze, brown, gold, orange	July & Aug.
Scabiosa (pincushion flower)	Summer	10 days	2'	blue, white	July & Aug.
Sedum spectabile	Summer	14–21 days	1½'	pink	Aug.-Sept.
Stokesia (Stokes aster)	Summer	21 days	1–2'	blue, white	July & Aug.

CHART 4.1

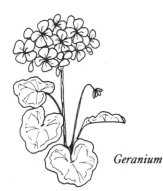

Geranium

Perennial Aster

Many perennial seeds have a tough seed coat and are just plain stubborn when it comes to germination. These include dictamnus, delphinium, certain rose species, and many others. You should stratify these seeds by mixing them with moist peat moss, sand, or vermiculite, and keeping the mix in a refrigerator for 2 or 3 months at 35 degrees F. This has the same effect as planting in a cold frame for the winter.

Biennials

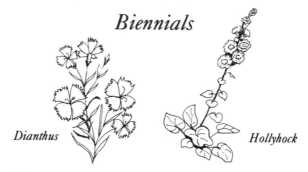

Dianthus   *Hollyhock*

Biennials are almost like perennials but they need two growing seasons to complete their life cycle. A biennial makes part of its growth one year, blooms the following year, sets seed, and dies. Examples include hollyhock, English daisy, Canterbury bells, foxglove, and sweet william. In warm areas these plants live and grow as perennials.

Most biennials are started in a seedbed or cold frame in June or July, although some are started in August. This gives a long enough season to grow good husky plants for blooms the following year. Biennials self-sow,

THE BEST-KNOWN BIENNIALS

Botanical Name	Common Name	Color	Height (in feet)	Bloom Date	When to sow
Althea rosea	Hollyhock	Various	6	July, August	Summer
Campanula medium	Canterbury bells	Blue, pink, white, purple	3	June, July	Late spring
Dianthus barbatus	Sweet william	Pink, white, red, lavender, two-tone	1–2	June, July, August	Spring
Digitalis purpurea	Foxglove	Lavender, peach, pink, purple, rose, white	3	June, July	Spring or summer
Lunaria annua	Honesty	Purple, white, rose, whitish blue	3	May, June	Spring or summer
Salvia sclarea	Clary	Pink, blue	3	July, August	Spring

CHART 4.2

so it's a good idea not to cultivate too vigorously around the plants if you want to save the seedlings. They are generally winter hardy and need little or any protection, but a cold frame or straw mulch helps to keep young plants through the winter. (See Chapter 1.)

HERBS AND SPROUTS

BECAUSE MORE PEOPLE THAN EVER ARE AVOIDING SALT IN their diets, they are using herbs as a health substitute. The twentieth-century cook has discovered the charm of homegrown herbs, and we see many herb plants in the garden or in pots in the windowsill. Homegrown herbs take us back beyond the present mechanized age, in which seasonings are purchased in packaged form at the supermarket, to the days when families relied on backyard gardens for seasonings that gave meals distinction. The early settlers in America brought with them seeds and cuttings of their favorite herbs, and we find replicas of their herb gardens at such treasured spots of colonial America as Mount Vernon, Wakefield, and Stratford.

COMMON HERBS

HERB	GREEN THUMB TIPS	OUTDOOR USES
ANGELICA	Start by seed or plants, grow in light shade. Sow in fall and transplant in spring.	Grows 6 ft. tall, ideal for background plant. Cut flower heads off after blooming for longer life.
ANISE	Plant seed in May in well-drained soil, full sun. Sow seed directly without transplanting.	2-ft. annual, sprawling and rather slow-growing.
BASIL	Sow seed in well-drained soil after frost. Likes full sun and ample water.	Border plant, 2 ft. tall. Attracts bees.
BORAGE	Sow seed in poor, dry soil, full sun. Thin to 12 in. apart.	3-ft. annual, star-shaped blue flowers. Good in rock garden.
CARAWAY	Sow seed in spring or fall in dry, light soil. Germination is slow.	2-ft. biennial, white flowers, useful in back border.
ENGLISH CHAMOMILE	Sow seed in spring or late summer in sunny spot, thin to 10 in. apart.	Hardy perennial, 12 in. tall. Useful in border or as ground cover.

INDOOR USES	HARVESTING & STORING
Use young leaves with fish, seed for cookies and candies.	Cut seed head before dry and keep in warm, airy place.
Fresh leaves in salads, soups, and stews. Seeds in cake, cookies, and fruit pies.	Pick fresh leaves as needed. For seed, clip flower clusters when gray-green and dry in attic.
Use fresh or dried leaves in eggs, meats, salads, and vegetables.	Cut 6 in. above ground when plants flower, and dry. Strip leaves and flower tips and store in opaque jars.
Teas and vegetables.	Use fresh. Pick flowers and leaves, dry and store in jars.
Seeds in meats, salads, soups, rye bread, and cookies.	Cut seed heads before dry and leave on cloth in attic. Store dried seed after separating.
Herb tea.	Cut flower heads in full bloom and dry in sun. Store in closed containers.

HERB	GREEN THUMB TIPS	OUTDOOR USES
CHERVIL	Sow seed in spring, grows best in shaded, moist spot. Thin to 4 in. apart.	Hardy annual, 2 ft. tall, handsome deep-green foliage. Ideal in back of border.
CHIVES	Sow seed in spring or fall, or use divisions. Likes full sun, loamy soil, indoors or outdoors. Divide clumps every 3 or 4 years.	Onion-like perennial, 12-in. clumps with lavender blooms. Good in rock gardens.
CORIANDER	Sow seed in late spring, 1 in. deep in well-drained soil, full sun. Thin to 1 foot apart.	Handsome annual, 12 in. tall. Do not disturb by cultivating.
DILL	Sow seed in spring or late fall in full sun. Do not transplant.	4-ft. annual which may need fencing for wind protection.
FENNEL	Sow in rows in May and thin to 6 in. apart. When plants are half-grown, draw earth up around them to blanch the bulbous stalk.	Grown as an annual. Common sweet fennel grows similarly.
HOREHOUND	Plant seeds or root divisions in spring. Takes poor soil, full sun	Coarse perennial, 2 ft. tall. forms bush for background use.

INDOOR USES	HARVESTING & STORING
Use fresh or dried as aromatic garnish, or use like parsley.	Cut leaves and dry quickly. Keep in tightly sealed glass jars.
Use in omelets, salads, cheese, appetizers, and soups.	Cut leaves as needed.
Meat, cheese, salads, soups, and pickles.	Snip stalks when seeds are ripe, dry in shade, then separate seeds and store in glass.
Heads in cheese, eggs, pickles. Seeds in soups, gravies, and vegetables.	Pick whole sprays and hang upside down to dry.
Valued for its anise-like flavor cooked or in salad.	Plants mature in 60 days and are then dug. Seeds of common fennel used in cookies, cheeses, and with vegetables.
Cakes, cookies, sauces, and meats.	Cut stems just before flowering, dry in shade, and store in opaque jars.

HERB	GREEN THUMB TIPS	OUTDOOR USES
LEMON BALM	Sow seed in summer, in full sun.	Hardy perennial, good border plant, 3 ft. tall. May be a pest if allowed to self-sow.
LEMON VERBENA	Start from cuttings in sand. Full sun and ample water.	Fine perennial, also good houseplant.
SWEET MARJORAM	Start early and transplant out in spring to dry, well-drained soil.	Annual, 15 in. high, with gray foliage, white flowers. Front border.
PARSLEY	Soak seed in warm water for a day; plant outdoors in rich soil, full sun.	Neat plant 12″ tall. Biennial. Curly or plain (Italian). Can bring indoors in fall, but produces only 1–2 months and then forms seeds. Best to make new sowing in pots.
PEPPERMINT	Plant seeds, roots, or runners in spring. Shade and wet soils are good.	Spreads fast, keep in bound with metal strips. Set in back border.
ROSEMARY	Start seed indoors in spring, or root cuttings. Likes full sun, poor, limy soil.	Perennial 4 ft. high, blue flowers. Needs winter protection.
SAGE	Start from seed or cuttings in spring. Full sun and drained soil. Mulch in winter, remove dead wood in spring.	Shrubby 2-ft. perennial, light blue flowers. Fine addition to border.

INDOOR USES	HARVESTING & STORING
Valuable in seasoning.	Cut tips 2 or 3 times a season. Store in opaque jars after drying.
Sachets, perfumes, toilet water. Flavors fruit salads, jellies, beverages.	Pick tender leaves and dry.
Eggs, sauces, soups, stuffings.	Use fresh, or dry leaves and store in opaque jars.
Use as garnish in egg dishes, meat sauces, salads. High in vitamins.	Cut as needed, or dry in oven and keep in tight jar.
Fresh or dried leaves in jellies, desserts, beverages.	Cut stems in bloom, dry and store in tight jars.
Fresh or dried leaves in poultry, meats, or seafoods.	Cut leaves just before blooming period, crush and store in tight container.
Chopped fresh leaves in cheese, pickles, or sausage. Powdered leaves in stuffings.	Cut young tips, dry over stove, pulverize leaves and store in tight jar.

HERB	GREEN THUMB TIPS	OUTDOOR USES
SAVORY, SUMMER	Sow seed in spring in loamy soil, full sun. Grows fast. Winter savory has same care and uses.	Annual, 18 in. high, bushy, pinkish flowers.
SHALLOT	Start from new shoots or cloves in spring. Rich, moist soil.	Bulbous annual without much ornamental value.
SPEARMINT	Same as for peppermint.	
SWEET CICELY	Plant seed in fall or spring, or divide parent plant. Partial shade, any type soil.	Fernlike leaves, fragrant white flowers, 2 to 3 ft. tall.
TARRAGON	Root cuttings in spring, well-drained soil, full sun or semi-shade. Divide every 2 or 3 years as plants get woody.	Handsome foliage enhances the border.

The word is pronounced "herb" or "erb" depending on where you live. The ideal location for the herb garden is near the house, where the plants will be handy to gather and easily tended and watered during dry weather. A 10-by-12-foot herb garden will supply the needs of the average family. In general, one short row or a few feet of row of each of the annual herbs and a half dozen plants of the perennials should be sufficient.

INDOOR USES	HARVESTING & STORING
Fresh leaves in green vegetables. Dried leaves in meats, turnips, or cabbage.	Pull up plant and dry, store leaves in sealed jars.
Use in same manner as onion.	Pull up when tops are yellow, dry 2 or 3 days. Cut off tops and store cloves in trays.
Seeds have spicy taste, used with other herbs.	Pick seeds when green.
Flavors sauces, salads, seafoods, stuffings.	Cut anytime and hang in loose bundles.

Starting Seeds Indoors

Most herb seed can be started indoors in pots of loose, humusy-rich soil such as a mixture of equal parts of sand, peat, and loam, or in a Peat-Lite–type mix. The number-one rule is not to sow the seed too thickly. After seedlings are about 1 inch tall they can be transplanted into 4- or 5-inch pots or grown together in 8-

or 10-inch pots. You can start herbs outdoors (see the accompanying herb chart), and then pot them in a clump in the fall and bring them indoors for winter use. Trim back old growth to encourage young shoots. Herbs like the brightest window possible, ample water, and a light feeding once a month or so.

Chart 5.1 lists some common herbs the home gardener should attempt to grow.

Edible Sprouts

One tablespoon of tiny seeds will fill a quart jar with sprouts.

Courtesy of Manna Supply Co.

The custom of sprouting seeds for food is more than twice as old as the Great Wall of China. Today the majority of Americans, once unfamiliar with sprouts, buy them in salad bars. If you are hungry for fresh vegetables during winter months, grow your own sprouts right in your own kitchen and enjoy their nutritional benefits. There are elaborate sprouting setups for sale, but any glass fruit jar will do.

What sprouting does to seeds is unbelievable! It stimulates many beneficial changes and boosts the nutritional quality during the few hours of sprouting. And the amazing thing is that no soil or plant food is needed—nothing but moisture and air and a warm spot under your kitchen sink. A tablespoon of tiny alfalfa seeds will grow into tender sprouts that jam themselves into every corner of a standard quart glass jar.

Part of the fun of sprouting seeds for food is trying out different kinds. Wheat sprouts have a nutlike flavor, but become chewy due to natural gluten in the wheat grain. Radish sprouts have a sharp radish zing and are excellent for jazzing up a green salad. Lentils have a gentle mild flavor of their own, as do mung beans, the old standby.

When buying seeds for sprouting, be sure the seeds are intended for food use; some seed intended for outdoor planting has been treated with a pesticide to protect young seedlings. Unless they have been so treated, most common vegetable seeds can be used for sprouting.

Your local health food store has a line of seeds for sprouting, as do many seed houses. Most sprouts will stay crisp for as long as a week in a refrigerator, but for maximum flavor and nutrition, sprout only what you can use in three or four days.

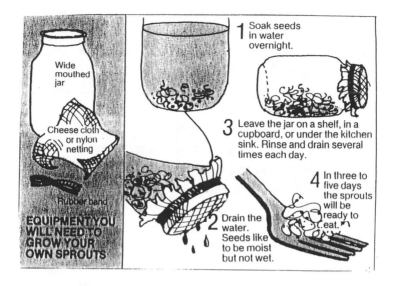

Sprouting seeds: If you want fresh, organic, enzyme-rich vegetables—winter or summer—without going to the market, try sprouting seeds.

Courtesy of Christian Science Monitor

Once you try sprouting, you'll never cease to wonder how amazing it is to grow so much nutrition with no insects, no insecticides, no artificial fertilizers—right in your kitchen cupboard or under the kitchen sink.

HOUSEPLANTS

MANY GARDENERS ARE BEGINNING TO EXPERIENCE great excitement and satisfaction from growing houseplants from seed. It's the cheapest way to build up a collection, and they are as easy to start as petunias, geraniums, coleus, and dozens of other annuals sold as bedding plants in the spring.

Number-one rule: Since most of us can accommodate only a few indoor plants, it's wise to limit the amount of seed ordered or sown. However, many church bazaars sell houseplants by the hundreds, so you may want to look into the possibility of sowing extra seed for raising plants to sell at bazaars, garage sales, etc. Most rules cited for sowing annuals from seeds apply to houseplants grown from seed. Pay close attention to soil mixes. You can sow any kind of houseplant seed in Peat-Lite–type mixes, of which there are many varieties, including Pro-Mix, Redi-Earth, and Jiffy-Mix. *Never* use soil from the garden for starting seed of houseplants or any other plants. The seedling mix should be moistened thoroughly before sowing.

Use any container that drains well, such as the fiber packs florists use. Fine seed should not be covered, but pressed lightly onto the mix with fingertips. Larger seed needs to be covered only deep enough so that it cannot be seen. Label each variety of seed sown, indicating date and source of seed, for your future information.

Since some seeds of houseplants are either rare, expensive, or in short supply, it is a good idea to sow only part of a packet, so that a portion of the seeds can be used in another sowing. Be sure to give seed enough time to germinate. Some varieties come up fast, and many take a week, some even a month or more. Don't be in too big a hurry to transplant houseplant seedlings. Allow the seedlings to grow until two or three true leaves show up, then transplant. Dig a clump out of the moistened seed box and separate each carefully so as not to sever roots. Move them into individual peat, clay, or plastic pots as you do annuals. Keep them in a bright light and add 25 percent-strength fertilizer once every 2 or 3 weeks. Never use dry fertilizer on houseplants.

After sowing, place the seed flat in a pan with about a half inch of water. Top watering is not recommended because it will displace seed. Misting with warm water is acceptable. As with annuals, put a plastic sheet or pane of glass over the seed and place it in a temperature of 72 degrees, *both day and night.*

The following chart provides germination time of some common houseplants in homes, in greenhouses, and under fluorescent lights. Most of these do well in a temperature 72 degrees F. both day and night.

Our thanks to Ted Marsten for help on this chart.

DAYS TO GERMINATION FOR SOME HOUSEPLANTS

Name of Plant	Greenhouse	Fluorescent Lights
Abutilon		18–21
Achimenes		15
Aeschynanthus		13
Alloplectus		30
Aloe species		8
Alstroemeria	15–30	
Amaryllis		30
Asarina	10	
Asparagus fern	60–80	18–30
Begonia "Calla Queen"		11
Begonia evansiana		7
Begonia rex	30	11
Begonia semperflorens	14–19	6
Begonia species	15–60	12–18
Begonia tuberous rooted	15–20	13

Name of Plant	Greenhouse	Fluorescent Lights
Bellonia spinosa		19
Billbergia	15	12
Browallia	15–20	10
Cacti	8	3
Calccolaria	15	
Calamondin		11
Calla lily	30–35	
Capsicum	12	
Cladanthus		2
Coleus	6–10	3
Columnea hybrids		9
Cordyline indivisa		13
Crossandra	21	
Cyclamen	42	
Eccremocarpus	9	
Epiphyllum, mixed		14
Episcia		14
Erythrina crista-galli	14 months	
Exacum affine	11	
Ficus elastica	15–20	
Ficus macrophylla	18	
Gesneria christii		14–20
Gesneria cuneifolia		10–15
Geranium (pelargonium)	4–9	
Gerbera	6–10	
Gloxinia (florists)		7
Gloxinia perennis		9–15
x Gloxinera "Cupid's Doll"		13–15

Name of Plant	Greenhouse	Fluorescent Lights
x Gloxinera "Pink Petite"		14
Hamatocactus setispinus	5	
Hypoestes	6	
Impatiens	7–14	6
Jacobinia	7–20	
Kalanchoe "Tom Thumb"	15	7–14
Kohleria species		12–20
Punica (dwarf)		7–10
Ruellia	5	
Saintpaulia		10–18
Sinningia pusilla		10
Sinningia "White Sprite"		10–15
Smithiantha		12–30
Solanum	10–16	
Strelitzia	20–40	
Streptocarpus (various species)		10–60
Streptocarpus "Constant Nymph"		15
Streptocarpus kirkii		14
Streptocarpus rexii hybrids		15
Succulents mixed	6–15	4

Cacti

In a desert, cactus seed have a small chance of survival. Millions are produced but most of them perish at the instant of germination. In a desert, as soon as an embryo cracks its seed coat, the tender seedling is exposed to one of the most hostile and harsh environments on earth. The chances of a seed landing where there is water, organic matter, and shade are few, but a few seeds do survive the tribulations of germination and grow. It is estimated that a giant saguaro cactus (*Carnegiea gigantea*) produces 12 million seeds during its lifetime. Of these, perhaps a single plant survives to reproduce its own kind.

You might think from this that the prospect of starting cacti from seed seems awfully futile. Why attempt such a feat if the success is so ridiculously slim? The truth is that cactus seeds fail in the wild because of a hostile environment, not because they are hard to start or grow. Given the best conditions of light, moisture, and temperature, cactus seeds germinate with a success rate of 75 to 100 percent. At that rate, they are comparable to radishes. So if you can start radishes, you can probably grow cacti.

Though the selection of cactus (and cactus seeds) is endless, if you're growing them from seed for the first time, we suggest you start with a barrel cactus (*Echinocactus*). Once you start growing cactus from seed, you're likely to become a compulsive collector!

Bill Taylor, a cactus specialist, starts his cactus plants in a four-tier light garden under 40-watt fluorescent tubes. (Incandescent lights, used alone, have the wrong spectral balance and are completely unsuitable.) He feels most kinds of tubes work well—even a combination of regular cool white and warm white. Some fluorescent tubes cause seedlings to elongate.

SOIL MIXTURE: Probably the trickiest part of growing cactus from seed is creating an appropriate soil. You need a porous, lightweight (and nourishing) growing medium. Scooping soil from the garden or sand from a bank is not advisable. There are many useful mixtures, but one we recommend consists of one part commercial Peat-Lite–type soil, one part fine or medium vermiculite, and one part finely ground washed sand (lumber yards sell it). Since desert soil tends to be alkaline, most cacti do not do well in a strongly acid mix. Low pH means high acidity, and many peat mixes have a pH reading from 4 to 5, so it's a good idea to add lime to make the soil more alkaline. If you add a half to 1 teaspoon of dolomitic limestone and the same amount of gypsum to an 8-by-12by-2½-inch pan of soil mix, you will raise the pH to 6.5 or 7, making it more alkaline or nearly neutral. Don't overdo the lime, since seedlings suffer if soil is too alkaline.

SOWING: You can sow cactus seed in fiber plant packs, aluminum pie tins, or any kind of container that holds at least 2½ inches of soil. Soil depth is important—if it's too shallow the pans may dry out too fast, and if it's too deep there is a chance of soil stagnation and wet or rotted roots.

Fine seed can be sown on the surface of the soil and dusted with a tiny amount of vermiculite or not. Dump some seed in the palm of your hand and with the thumb and forefinger of the other hand lift a few seed and rotate them gently onto the soil mix. Some experts use a pair of tweezers to deposit the seed. Seeds of larger varieties need about 1 inch between seeds. Keep soil moist and the temperature between 70 and 80 degrees F. day and night.

Larger seeds, which produce a powerful taproot, may have the tendency to rise out of the soil if the roots hit an obstacle forcing them upward. Firm the plants back in with your fingers, or take a knife and edge them back in.

Be sure to label each seed you plant.

Bonsai

There's new interest in the subject of bonsai (pronounced bone-SIGH), a technique for growing dwarfed living plants. The Japanese are masters at the art, although many Americans are now enthusiastic about it. Some firms offer a starter kit that contains everything you need to get going in the bonsai business.

The art of bonsai was begun over 500 years ago in Japan (or perhaps China), and interest in it grew in the United States after World War II. If you're interested in knowing more about bonsai, contact the American Bonsai Society. Write to: Executive Secretary, Box 358, Keene, NH 03431. The society will tell you the best seeds to buy and start for your bonsai collection.

TREES AND SHRUBS

MANY TREES AND SHRUBS CAN BE GROWN FROM SEEDS, nuts, and cones, which can be collected during autumn walks through native woods and fields.

Most trees and shrubs have a built-in protective mechanism called dormancy. This insures that the seeds do not grow before they are able to mature into plants. Premature sprouting in the fall could cause seedlings to die in the winter. Sprouting must occur in the spring so the plant will have a long season of favorable growing conditions and be established enough to survive the next winter.

Several different factors encourage seed germination at the proper time. Seeds of the walnut, hickory, locust, and other trees have hard seed coverings; the embryo cannot grow until moisture gets to it. In order for sprouting to take place this covering or shell must either split or disintegrate. Germination can be speeded up by filing a little notch in the seed coat with a file or nicking the coat with a knife so water can get inside.

Many tree and shrub seeds require chilling before they can germinate. This applies to many in temperate northern zones. Most respond to temperatures around 32 degrees F. The length of the chilling period varies, however most species need only one period. Nuts or seeds that would normally drop to the ground in fall could be planted in a cold frame after they have been gathered. Most evergreen seeds from cones are among the easiest to grow. Seeds of flowering shrubs, such as roses, are a fascinating challenge.

Our good friend Dr. Ray Rothenberger of the Department of Horticulture, University of Missouri, has given us these tips on growing trees and shrubs from seeds:

"Some seeds have an incompletely developed embryo at the time they drop from the plant. They should not be chilled until the embryo has developed fully. The required warm period is called after-ripening. Some hollies, ash, and ginkgo have such requirements.

"The pulp that surrounds seeds often contains inhibitors that prevent germination. Therefore, when you grow seeds from fleshy fruits, remove this pulp before the seeds are planted. If it is not removed an extra year may be needed for germination.

"This is not nearly a complete explanation of what seeds need to germinate. However, anyone gathering seeds for fall planting should be aware that such needs do exist. Most seeds should be planted directly after harvest. In some seeds additional dormancy will develop as seeds dry. Other seeds are easily killed by excessive drying.

"Normally, fall planting outdoors is the easiest way to achieve all these conditions, particularly when precise details are unknown. Provide tree and shrub seeds with a good seedbed in a protected location that is well marked. Remember that you may wait for several seasons before the seedlings emerge."

Contact your College of Agriculture Department of Ornamental Horticulture for information about growing trees and shrubs from seed native to your area.

Citrus and Other Mild Climate Fruits

Citrus fruits such as oranges, lemons, limes, tangerines, grapefruit, calamondins, etc., can be started from seed, but don't count on the plant to produce fruit with the same flavor as that you buy in stores. However, you'll get wild ("common") fruit with lots of nice glossy foliage and sweet-smelling flowers. If you want edible citrus fruits buy the plants already budded onto rootstock in the nursery.

For starting seeds, use a Peat-Lite–type mix or Jiffy-7's pellets. Keep seeds moist and at 70 degrees F. or above. Seeds germinate quickly if they have been taken from truly ripe fruits.

OLIVES: Select seed of black olives that have not been processed with heat. Scar each seed carefully with a file, making a small opening in the seed coat. Put three seeds in a 5-inch pot of Peat-Lite–type soil mix and keep moist at around 70 degrees F. Olive seeds are very slow to germinate, so be patient.

DATES: These are a challenge to start and grow from seed. However, this palm, native to desert regions, makes a fine houseplant. The bony seed must be notched with a file to make a tiny hole through the seed coat. Place seed horizontally in peat lite mix or Jiffy-7's pellets that have been moistened thoroughly. Keep moist and at 80 degrees F. for good germination. They take from 3 to 6 weeks to show a small leaf.

KIWI FRUIT: Although not a tropical fruit, the kiwi that is sold commercially is from a mild, temperate climate and cannot stand frost. This should not stop the curious gardener from starting its seed; they make an attractive vine for a houseplant. There are hardy small-fruited types handled by some nurseries. Their fruit is much less tasty and bearing is unpredictable. Sexes are separate on both hardy and nonhardy types, so plant both male and female vines.

Seeds from kiwi fruit are tiny. Using a table knife, lift clusters of seeds from the fruit and spread them on waxed paper. After a few days, separate them and press them down gently on a Peat-Lite–type mix. Set the pot in the refrigerator after moistening it thoroughly and covering it with plastic wrap.

Although we have had kiwi seeds germinate in 4 weeks without giving them a cool treatment, a larger percentage will sprout if they are planted and then stored in a refrigerator for 4 to 5 weeks. Seeds must not dry out; keep them moist, not wet. After the cool treatment, move them to a warm spot (about 70 degrees F.). Transplant when seedlings are about 2 inches high.

There are many other tropical and semitropical fruits to challenge the inveterate seed starter, so try others, too. Most require the same conditions as citrus seeds.

Deciduous Fruits and Nuts

You can start certain fruit trees (apple, pear, cherry, plum, etc.) from seed, but in most cases the fruit will be "common" or wild—hardly fit to eat. Unless you merely want to experiment and find out just what kind of fruit comes from seed-started trees, the process is not worth the trouble. A good eating apple variety is the result of planting probably 50,000 seeds and selecting only the best. It takes years to produce an edible apple from seed. And it takes time for seedlings to reach bearing age so they can be tested. So if you want to grow good fruit, buy grafted or budded stock from your nursery. You can be sure the grafted or budded fruit will be true to name. If started from seed, the chances are 1 in 50,000 that a variety will be fit to eat.

There are exceptions to this rule, however. If you plant peach pits (seeds) you may get a variety of peach that's as tasty as some budded or grafted types. However, it may or may not have hardiness, vigor, or other desirable qualities of the parent tree.

Most seeds of fruit grown in northern temperate areas can be started in a cold frame with a mix of sand, peat moss, and garden loam.

Most nut trees can be started from seed. The secret is to plant the nuts immediately after harvesting. You can do this in a cold frame or directly in the ground (protect the nuts from rodents with hardware cloth). Here they get a cold treatment known as "stratification" (see page xx); a physiological change takes place in the seed during its exposure to temperatures about 3 or 4 degrees F. above freezing. Stratification can be achieved by storing nuts in a refrigerator for 6 to 8 weeks in a small plastic bag filled with peat moss.

If you are interested in growing first-quality nuts, our advice is to buy budded or grafted nut trees from your nursery. Otherwise, take a chance and grow seedlings from a selected strain of your favorite nut tree. Keep in mind that trees started from seed show great variation in their hardiness, vigor, yield, and quality.

WILDFLOWERS

ONE OF THE FASTEST-GROWING SEGMENTS OF THE HOR-
ticultural world is wildflower gardening. There are several good seed houses that sell wildflower seeds; among
them are Applewood Seed, W. Atlee Burpee Company,
Comstock Ferre & Company, Gurney Seed & Nursery,
Nichols Garden Nursery, Park Seed Company, Rocky
Mountain Seed Co., Johnny's Selected Seeds, Vaughan
Seed Company, and many other good firms. Be sure to
follow their directions.

CAUTION: Before you sow seed in your front lawn
make sure you are not violating any zoning order. Many
neighbors, especially in affluent suburbs, may not see

the beauty in wildflowers and say they are an eyesore that will draw rodents and will spread to other yards via airborne seeds. We've seen many cases where neighbors complain to city officials who define zoning laws which call for "appropriate landscaping." A wildflower lawn in the middle of well-groomed lawns just doesn't sit well with some neighbors and city officials.

Steve Atwood of Clyde Robin Seed Company gave us these good tips on wildflower gardening.

TIPS ON SOIL PREPARATION: In warmer climates where there is no frost, plant seeds in fall (preferably October). In colder climates, plant them in the spring after the last frost. Remove "competition" (weeds and grasses) from your planting area, and start with a clean seedbed. Loosen the soil to a depth of a few inches by raking it or turning it over lightly with a shovel.

The old adage "What you put in you get out" applies here. You can plant wildflower seeds without preparing the soil ahead of time, but your wildflowers may be sparse as a result.

TIPS ON PLANTING THE SEED: Scatter seeds evenly over the seedbed. This is easier to do if you first mix your wildflower seed with sand (1 part seed to 4 parts sand). Once you've scattered your seeds, lightly rake the area or sprinkle the area with just enough water to "melt" the soil down over the seeds.

Do not cover the seeds with a heavy layer of soil. They should be covered just enough to keep them hidden from birds or other predators and to keep them from blowing away before they take hold.

(And this from Dr. Ray Rothenberger: "Wildflowers such as bloodroot and trillium have the most complex requirements to break dormancy. They require 4 to 6 months of cold, followed by 4 to 6 months of warm while the roots develop, then 4 to 6 months of more cold for the plant shoot to break dormancy. This total process may require 2 to 3 years from the time the seed drops, depending on weather conditions during the process.")

TIPS ON CARING FOR YOUR SEEDBED:
Once your seeds are planted, most of your work is done. If you plant during the rainy season, you can just sit back and let nature take over. If you plant in spring or summer after the rainy season, you must provide water for your newly planted seeds. The trick is to keep them moist for at least 14 days.

After those first two critical weeks, tiny green shoots will begin to appear. If your soil had weeds in it before you planted your wildflower seeds, you're likely to see some weed sprouts along with your wildflower plants. Learn to identify the weeds, if you can, and pull them out as they occur.

Watch for blossoms 45 to 90 days after germination. Depending on the area and variety of seed, plants will bloom for 45 to 60 days. If you've planted a mix, you'll see your flower change over the course of several weeks, as some flowers come on strong and then fade as other varieties burst into bloom.

AFTER THE BLOOMING SEASON: When the flowers are finished blooming you can do several things. If they are on a hillside, just let the flowers go to seed. They will decompose with the winter rains and the seeds will germinate and flower again in spring. Should you want a more uniform look, mow the flowers down to 4 inches after they have gone to seed and the seed has dropped. This way you will have flowers back again next spring. If you cut your flowers before they have gone to seed, you will kill them.

When your flowers finish blooming, they will begin to "set seed." If you want another flower show next year, let them die back naturally. If you want to collect seed (for next year) from the heavy seeders (the annuals), check on the seed pods once a week after the plants have appeared to die back. When the seed has turned dark, it's dry and ready to collect. Store it in labeled envelopes.

CHILDREN'S INDOOR GARDENS

CHILDREN LOVE THE EXCITEMENT OF WATCHING SEEDS produce flowers, vegetables, and even trees. There are countless miniature gardens that can be made from the simplest household articles. Here are a few projects to keep kids busy, especially on rainy days.

Ball of Green

Soak a large, coarse sponge, then sprinkle it with clover, grass, or mustard seeds (the kinds you pick up in the spice department of the grocery store). Then hang the sponge in a bright window. It must be kept damp at all times; spray it with a spritzer at least once a day. Before long, seeds will sprout and cover the sponge with a solid coating of greenery.

Growing Oak Trees from Acorns

In the fall, gather acorns. Take them home and plant them about an inch deep in pots of soil mix that is one part each of sand, peat moss, and loam (garden soil), or use one of the Peat-Lite–type mixes. Keep the medium moist. Though they may take a few weeks to break through their hard seed coat, acorns will sprout with no special treatment. They will grow into fine seedling trees that can be given away as gifts. We think they are a nice gift on the occasion of the birth of a child, as they can be planted as a memento.

Pixie Pie Plate

Cut a piece of flannel to fit inside a large pie plate. Saturate the flannel with water and sprinkle some tiny seeds on it, such as any kind of grass seed mixture. Place the plate in a bright, warm (about 70 to 75 degrees F.) window. If kept damp, the seeds will grow practically before your eyes.

Green Pastures

Pack moist earth or a Peat-Lite–type mix into a wide shallow cake pan. Sow it with grass seed, then put a

Try growing a pasture in a pan by sowing grass and other tiny seeds. Be creative!—add a mirror for a pond and matchsticks for a bridge.

sprinkling of vermiculite on top. Moisten thoroughly with a sprinkler or spritzer. Place pan in a bright window, and keep the mix moistened. When the surface is covered with green, let children place miniature animals and buildings in the "pasture." A little mirror (like those in cosmetic compacts) makes a great make-believe pond.

Miniature Citrus Orchards

There are many items from the shopping bag that can be used to grow plants for youngsters. Orange, lemon, grapefruit, and tangerine seeds sprout and grow readily in Peat-Lite–type mixes. (See "Starting Citrus and Other Mild Climate Fruits in Chapter 7.)

Avocados Show Their Roots

An avocado pit is a great seed to start in a transparent glass with water. In this way, children can see roots grow. Put the "dimple" down in the water after toothpicks have been spaced around the middle (see drawing). Be sure fruit is ripe and at room temperature or the pit won't sprout.

The avocado (Alligator pear) has a big seed or pit which can be used to start an avocado tree. Watch them sprout in a jar of water.

APPENDIX

Seed Companies

Bountiful Gardens
Ecology Action
5798 Ridgewood Road
Willits, CA 95490

Large selection of
vegetables, herbs, grains,
and cover crops. Supplies
for organic gardeners.

W. Atlee Burpee Company
Warminster, PA 18991

One of the largest seed
companies serving the
home gardener.

Clyde Robin Seed Company
Castro Valley, CA 94546

Large selection of
wildflowers and
perennials.

The Cook's Garden
P.O. Box 65
Londonderry, VT 05148

Many superior varieties of
vegetables, some of which
are European.

The Country Garden
Box 455A
Route 2
Crivitz, WI 54114

Specializes in flowers for cutting, many of which are edible.

DeGiorgi Company, Inc.
P.O. Box 413
Council Bluffs, IA 51502

Many Italian varieties of vegetables, some of unusual color.

Farmer Seed & Nursery
Faribault, MN 55021

General seed selection.

Henry Field's Seed & Nursery Company
Shenandoah, IA 51602

General seed selection.

Gleckler's Seedmen
Metamora, OH 43540

Standard vegetable seeds and many unusual varieties.

Good Seed
P.O. Box 702
Tonasket, WA 98855

Open-pollinated varieties of vegetables. Large list of beans, amaranth, cabbages, and corn.

Gurney Seed & Nursery Company
Yankton, SD 57079

Large selection of flower and vegetable seeds.

Halcyon Gardens Herbs
P.O. Box 124-M
Gibsonia, PA 15044

Large selection of herb seeds.

Harris Seeds
60 Saginaw Dr.
Box 22960
Rochester, NY 14624-2960

Standard flower and vegetable varieties and some herbs.

Hastings
434 Marietta Street NW
P.O. Box 4274
Atlanta, GA 30302

Vegetable varieties for the South.

Heirloom Gardens
P.O. Box 138
Guerneville, CA 95446

Large number of open-pollinated varieties of vegetables and many herbs.

Herb Gathering, Inc.
5742 Kenwood
Kansas City, MO 64110

Mainly seed from France, including French varieties of sorrel, chamomile, Alpine strawberries, dwarf basil, and other herbs.

Horticultural Enterprises
P.O. Box 810082
Dallas, TX 75381

A specialist in peppers, this nursery carries thirty varieties of sweet and hot peppers, as well as tomatillos, jicama, and epazote.

J. L. Hudson, Seedsman
P.O. Box 1058
Redwood City, CA 94064

Wide selection of different types of vegetables. Has flowers and herbs also.

Johnny's Selected Seeds
Foss Hill Road
Albion, ME 04910

Specializes in vegetable seeds for northern climates. Many Oriental varieties as well.

J. W. Jung Seed Company
Randolph, WI 53957

General seed catalog. Large selection of vegetables.

Kitazawa Seed Company
1748 Laine Avenue
Santa Clara, CA 95051

Specializes in seed for Oriental vegetables.

LeJardin du Gourmet
West Danville, VT 05873

Large selection of French vegetables, plus herbs.

Le Marché
Seeds International
P.O. Box 190
Dixon, CA 95620

Specializes in superior vegetables. Many varieties from Europe and Japan.

Lockhart Seeds, Inc.
P.O. Box 1361
3 North Wilson Way
Stockton, CA 95205

Large list of vegetable seeds. Great number of onion varieties.

Logee's Greenhouses
55 North Street
Danielson, CT 06239

Specializes in ornamentals and houseplants.

Long Island Seed and Plant
P.O. Box 1285
Riverhead, NY 11901

Interested in seed saving, heirloom vegetables, and self-sufficient living.

Earl May Seed & Nursery
Company
Shenandoah, IA 51603

Large selection of all kinds of seeds.

Meredith Seeds
16545 N.W. Germantown
Road
Portland, OR 97231

Compact and dwarf varieties of vegetables for small gardens, patios, and indoor gardens.

Native Seeds Search
3950 West New York Drive
Tucson, AZ 85745

Large selection of native Southwest vegetables and varieties grown by Native Americans. Membership.

Price list available to nonmembers.

Nichols Garden Nursery
1190 North Pacific Highway
Albany, OR 97321

Extensive list of herbs (plants as well as seeds) and unusual vegetables.

Park Seed Company
Cokesbury Road
Greenwood, SC 29647

One of the major suppliers of vegetable and flower seeds in the United States. Many varieties for small gardens.

Pepper Gal
10536 119th Avenue N
Largo, FL 33543

Large selection of seeds of hot and sweet peppers only.

Pinetree Garden Seeds
New Gloucester, ME 04260

Large selection of

vegetable seeds sold in inexpensive small packets.

Redwood City Seed Company
P.O. Box 361
Redwood City, CA 94064

Carries seeds of many unusual plants. Specializes in vegetable and herb seeds from Europe, Mexico, and the Orient.

Richters
Goodwood, Ontario
Canada LOC 1A0

Herb seed specialist carrying many unusual varieties.

Seeds for the World

See Vermont Bean Seed Company.

Seed Savers Exchange
Kent Whealy, Director
P.O. Box 70
Decorah, IA 52101

Devoted to saving heirloom varieties of vegetables. Membership fee includes large quarterly newsletter and list of seeds available for trade among members.

Seeds Blum
Idaho City Stage
Boise, ID 83706

Seeds of ornamental, heirloom, and open-pollinated vegetables. Catalog gives good information on seed saving, edible flowers, and landscaping with ornamental vegetables.

Shepherd's Garden Seeds
7389 West Zayante Road
Felton, CA 95018

Specializes in seeds of superior European vegetables and herbs selected for vigor and flavor. Many varieties unavailable through other seed companies.

Southern Exposure Seed Exchange
P.O. Box 158
North Garden, VA 22959

Interested in family heirlooms, popular hybrids, and varieties best suited to the mid-Atlantic region. Vegetables, herbs and some flowers.

Stokes Seeds, Inc.
P.O. Box 548
Buffalo, NY 14240

Large seed company. Carries a vast collection of vegetable and flower varieties, especially for northern gardens.

Sunrise Enterprises
P.O. Box 10058
Elmwood, CT 06110

Specializes in Oriental vegetables and herbs.

Tater Mater Seeds
R.R. 2
Wathena, KA 66090

Carries unusual selection of seeds, including Native American corns and uncommon tomato varieties of the company's own breeding.

Territorial Seed Company
P.O. Box 27
Lorane, OR 97451

A regional seed company specializing in vegetable varieties for the maritime Northwest.

Thompson & Morgan, Inc.
P.O. Box 1308
Jackson, NJ 08527

A British seed company specializing in unusual vegetables and flowers.

Tomato Growers Supply Company
P.O. Box 2237
Fort Myers, FL 33902

Over one hundred varieties of tomatoes, plus supplies for tomato

growers.

Tsang & Ma International
P.O. Box 294
Belmont, CA 94002

Large selection of Chinese vegetable seeds.

Twilley Seed Company
P.O. Box f65
Trevose, PA 19047

Many vegetable varieties for the home gardener, as well as flowers.

Vermont Bean Seed Company
Garden Lane
Fair Haven, VT 05743

Specializes in beans, but carries seeds of other vegetables, as well as seeds of herbs and flowers.

Wyatt-Quarles
Box 739
Garner, NC 27529

Vegetable varieties suited

to the South.

Dr. Yoo Farm
P.O. Box 290
College Park, MD 20740

Specializes in Oriental
vegetable varieties.

INDEX